Grace and Glory in One Another's Faces

Grace and Glory in One Another's Faces

Preaching and Worship

Ann Loades, CBE

Edited by Stephen Burns

CANTERBURY
PRESS
Norwich

Published in 2020 by Canterbury Press
Editorial office
3rd Floor, Invicta House,
108–114 Golden Lane,
London EC1Y 0TG, UK
www.canterburypress.co.uk

Canterbury Press is an imprint of Hymns Ancient & Modern Ltd
(a registered charity)

Hymns Ancient & Modern® is a registered trademark of
Hymns Ancient & Modern Ltd
13A Hellesdon Park Road, Norwich,
Norfolk NR6 5DR, UK

British Library Cataloguing in Publication data

A catalogue record for this book is available
from the British Library

978 1 78622 287 9

Typeset by Regent Typesetting
Printed and bound by
CPI Group (UK) Ltd

Contents

Kindness and Clout

STEPHEN BURNS

Calendar and lectionary

This collection gathers a range of sermons and addresses by Ann Loades. Rather than being presented chronologically, from the earliest piece (in the early 1980s) to the latest piece (in the late 2010s), they are clustered in two groups. Sermons in Part 1 were preached after Bible readings at Sunday morning Eucharists, in churches of and beyond Ann's own Anglican tradition. Others were preached in cathedrals in England, Scotland and further afield – sometimes at Eucharists, sometimes at matins or evensong. Others again were preached in contexts where evensong still prevails and even flourishes – university college chapels – with sermons here from such settings as Cambridge and Durham and Oxford and St Andrews.

If not taking up issues or themes suggested in the pattern of Bible readings in a lectionary, a number of the sermons that follow draw on another pattern in Christian liturgy – the calendar of saints, or *sanctorale*. Part 2 of this collection takes in a sweep of figures from the calendar.

To these sermons and addresses given in the setting of worship of one kind or another, *Grace and Glory in One Another's Faces* then adds two addresses *about* worship and preaching, delivered in different forums: to musicians, readers, clergy and others who in their turn preach and lead worship. Gathered at the centre are some key reflections on worship, beginning with the surprisingly neglected question 'Why worship?', followed by

'Word and sacrament', in which the preacher in this book articulates her understanding of preaching.

The voice of this preacher

Ann Loades was the first woman to be president of the Society for the Study of Theology. She was the first woman to be honoured with a CBE (Commander of the British Empire) medal for 'services to theology'.[1] She was the first woman in any discipline to be given a personal chair (professorship) at Durham University, where she taught in the Department of Theology from 1975 to 2003.[2] So she has achieved some significant 'firsts'.

Ann's workplace at Durham was clearly very important to her, and evidently one in which she did not always face or feel the discrimination stacked against women in the churches.[3] At the university, she not only taught candidates for ordination from the Church of England, Methodist Church and Roman Catholic Church, she was herself very much involved in church, albeit while refusing some of its presumptions about gender, serving for a time on the Doctrine Commission of the Church of England as well as other national bodies (notably, the Working Group on Women in the Episcopate). She also preached regularly, both near and far from Durham and in and beyond the Church of England (note that several of the sermons collected here were preached in Methodist assemblies, others in the Church of Scotland, and especially that since starting an active retirement in St Andrews she has been a member of the Scottish Episcopal Church). Through her decades in

---

1 And only the second person to receive such, C. F. D. Moule being the first.

2 For a longer introduction to Ann Loades' work, see Stephen Burns, 'Ann Loades (1938–)', in Stephen Burns, Bryan Cones and James Tengatenga, eds, *Twentieth-Century Anglican Theologians: From Evelyn Underhill to Esther Mombo* (Chichester: Wiley-Blackwell, 2020), 157–66.

3 Ann Loades, 'Introductory Address', *Feminist Theology* 3 (1993): 12–22, 12.

Durham itself, Ann sometimes preached in the cathedral, then her 'home church' and also the place where she became one of the first two people (elected together) made lay members of Chapter (the governing body) for that ancient place of worship – a building widely regarded as 'Britain's favourite'.[4] Here, then, was an ecclesial 'first'. And while the presence of women in the Church's leadership and pulpits may not now always seem so remarkable, it should be recalled that women were ordained priest in the Church of England only a year before Ann was made professor, in 1994 (and bishops only in 2015), and that in the Roman Catholic tradition to this day women may not formally 'preach' to a Sunday assembly – and nor can it always be presumed that women can in the Anglican tradition around the world.[5]

Durham was also the place where Ann became the first *Anglican* woman to be made professor of theology in an English university. This was the same university where she had studied as an undergraduate and then postgraduate, and then worked in pastoral and administrative roles (at St Mary's and Collingwood colleges), before she competed for her lectureship in the Department of Theology in 1975. Ann's first teaching position was in philosophy of religion. Her first rounds of publications were on Immanuel Kant (1724–1804) and various figures in eighteenth- and nineteenth-century thought, notably Coleridge (1772–1834), with both Kant and Coleridge key figures in her doctoral thesis.[6]

---

4 Jonathan Glancey, 'The votes are in: your favourite British building', *The Guardian*, 16 September 2011, www.theguardian.com/artanddesign/2011/sep/16/britains-best-building-readers-vote-results (accessed 20/08/20).

5 The latter point is vivid from my perspective from Australia, where the Diocese of Sydney does not ordain women as priests; Sydney is allied to numerous other dioceses and together these have the majority in General Synod, and the whole is conservatizing.

6 See Ann Loades, *Kant and Job's Comforters* (Newcastle: Avero, 1985) and for a detailed list of publications (up to 2008), the bibliography in Natalie Watson and Stephen Burns, eds, *Exchanges of Grace: Essays in Honour of Ann Loades* (London: SCM Press, 2008), 276–84.

Some of Ann's first work on figures from the twentieth century included attention to Simone Weil (1909–43), specifically in ways that linked to worship: Ann developed a critique of Weil's self-destructive preoccupation with the Eucharist, which was then amplified in a robust chapter, 'Why Certain Forms of Holiness are Bad for You', in her first book on feminist theology, *Searching for Lost Coins*.[7] That particular book was the first monograph on feminist theology to emerge from an academic in a British university theology department, and was the result of an invitation to offer the Scott Holland Lectures, paying particular attention to 'the significance of gender' within those lectures' wider concern with 'the religion of the Incarnation in its bearing on the social and economic life of man'. It was feminist theology for which she became best known, with *Searching for Lost Coins* followed up by the best-selling *Feminist Theology: A Reader*, a book that galvanized the challenge of feminist voices from around the North Atlantic.[8] That was followed by *Feminist Theology: Voices from the Past*,[9] which focused on the ground-breaking work of three women – Mary Wollstonecraft (1759–97) in the eighteenth century, Josephine Butler (1828–1906) in the nineteenth century, and Dorothy L. Sayers (1893–1957) in the twentieth century – each of whose work had not, in Ann's view, received the full recognition it deserved. Along with Evelyn Underhill (1875–1941), C. S. Lewis (1898–1963) and Austin Farrer (1904–68), Sayers has been a key focus of Ann's work on twentieth-century figures. Farrer was commonly recognized as one of the greatest preachers of his time; Sayers was no preacher but made highly innovative use of theatre (plays for cathedrals) and radio (most notably *The Man Born to be King*); Underhill, also not a preacher, was nevertheless a leading thinker on worship

---

7 Ann Loades, *Searching for Lost Coins: Explorations in Christianity and Feminism* (London: SPCK, 1987).

8 Ann Loades, ed., *Feminist Theology: A Reader* (London: SPCK, 1990), complemented by Ursula King, ed., *Feminist Theology from the Third World: A Reader* (London: SPCK, 1991).

9 Ann Loades, *Feminist Theology: Voices from the Past* (Oxford: Polity Press, 2000).

in her day as well as the first woman to address a gathering of the clergy of the Church of England and leader of many spiritual retreats in which she addressed audiences on mystical matters.[10] Underhill, it might also be noted, did write *about* preachers, perhaps most strikingly in a memorial of her own parish priest. Underhill's work stressed the importance of the life, spirit and style (she called it 'holiness') of the preacher as much as the voice, suggesting that many people did not come to church to listen to Father Wainright (her vicar) give sermons ('indifferent', 'inarticulate'!), but to 'look at his face', to 'be in his atmosphere'.[11] Crucially, it was what he communicated beyond words, in his person, that was most compelling.

All of this shapes what follows, in the explorations and urgings of the church- and college-based preaching on Sundays and the commendation of a skein of saints, as well as the texts about worship at the centre of this collection. And wide-ranging though those sermons and addresses may be, readers will find some consistent emphases running through them.

First, registering the titles of Ann's works mentioned above is important for understanding her approach not only to preaching but to the convictions she made manifest across her thinking and writing. 'Voices from the past' begins to suggest her interest in *listening*, giving close attention to Christian tradition, from which she draws some clear verdicts: tradition is by no means 'the dead hand of the past' but a most lively resource for levering open perspectives that a merely contemporary mindset might well miss.[12] Then, 'searching for lost coins' alludes not only to listening to the tradition but to a quest to revive what

---

10 See Ann Loades, *Evelyn Underhill* (London: Fount, 1997) and Ann Loades, 'Evelyn Underhill (1875–1941): Mysticism and Worship', *International Journal for the Study of the Christian Church* (2010): 57–70.

11 Evelyn Underhill, 'Father Wainright, 1848–1929', in Dana Greene, ed., *Evelyn Underhill: Modern Guide to the Ancient Quest for the Holy* (Albany, NY: SUNY Press, 1988), 193–6.

12 Ann Loades, 'Finding New Sense in the Sacramental', in Geoffrey Rowell and Christine Smith, eds, *The Gestures of God: Explorations in Sacramentality* (London: Continuum, 2004), 161–72, 164.

has been neglected – perhaps silenced or sidelined – and needs to be recovered, because precious and important.

Second, this searching is directed not only towards Scripture and tradition but also towards contemporaries. Ann is keen to stress how divine goodness should be reflected towards the neglected, undervalued, overlooked – those 'lost coins' too. For Ann, such concern is exemplified in Josephine Butler's tireless work for the abolition of the oppressive Contagious Diseases Acts – acts that worked against all women but especially those who were among the most vulnerable women of her day, sex workers (see the sermon on Butler below).[13] A number of sermons and addresses here add further examples, extra precedents, and more embodied sources of inspiration: perhaps most remarkably Catherine of Siena (1347–80), on the one hand writing as she did to pope and kings that their policies and practices were appalling, and on the other courageously putting her faith into action in the streets (at the gallows, in fact) in scenarios that were acutely demanding – 'almost overwhelming', as Ann says in her sermon.

Third, Catherine of Siena, Josephine Butler and their ilk may each in their own way approximate to what Ann calls in a sermon here 'the reign of God in our affairs' by refusing to kowtow to convention and supposed 'authorities' and to accept the status quo – and indeed Ann has noted in various places that 'obedience' is not necessarily a Christian virtue. For Ann, this is especially necessary when contending with ways in which the tradition – including its scriptural sources – has created some of the problems (not least for women) that need to be tackled. So Ann does not take the view that the Gospels (or Scripture at large) depict some panacea that needs to be retrieved. Rather, as she states in an essay on women in the episcopate, it must bluntly be said that the persistent biblical view that women are 'at fault' unless under the authority of males not only infects the wider tradition, but is flatly 'mistaken'.[14] For Ann, the witness of Scripture is complex, and getting to grips with its legacy

---

13 See also Loades, *Voices from the Past*.

14 Ann Loades, 'Women in the Episcopate?', *Anvil* (2004): 113–19, 114.

means acknowledging ambiguities as well as potential. As she succinctly describes the challenge: it means 'struggl[ing] hard with the devaluation of women for which the Christian tradition is in its own way responsible, [while] ... assum[ing] that the tradition also contains resources for transformation and change, despite the weight of criticism levelled against it'.[15]

Fourth, *Searching for Lost Coins* also states a conviction, found in practice throughout this book too, that Ann does 'not conceive resources for theological reflection in too narrow terms'.[16] This too is a dimension of searching, listening. So whatever focus there might be on the Bible in these sermons and addresses, there is also a breadth and largesse of attention. Neglected and undervalued persons have already been mentioned, but there is more: a looking far and wide, considering many perspectives, with all sorts of dialogue at play. Echoes of and engagements with novels and poetry are prominent, and given that among the other genres in which they worked, Sayers, Underhill and Lewis had each written novels,[17] and Sayers had translated the poetry of Dante Alighieri (c. 1265–1321) – his *Divine Comedy* – they may likely have conspired to give impetus for Ann's own wide-ranging explorations.

Fifth, and linked with refusal to kowtow, and also perhaps inspired by Dorothy L. Sayers' own combative approach distilled in the title of her book *Unpopular Opinions*, Ann is not afraid to state her mind. In an era in which popular approaches to pastoral care are sometimes charged with 'therapeutic captivity', and much discussion of worship has associated some liturgical styles with 'entertainment' (a dynamic that might be found not only in worship in cinemas, dancing to crap-rock, but also audiences attending choral services mainly 'for the music'), Ann typically advances a striking no-nonsense approach. Recurring challenges call for (and, it must be

15 Loades, *Voices from the Past*, 5.

16 Loades, *Searching*, 15.

17 See Ann Loades, 'Evelyn Underhill (1875–1941): Mysticism in Fiction', in Judith Maltby and Alison Shell, eds, *Anglican Women Novelists: From Charlotte Bronte to P. D. James* (London: T & T Clark, 2019).

added, repeatedly assure of the capacity for) sheer grit, sturdy *ascesis* (and there's a sermon on 'Saying No'), the discipline to persist at good though difficult things, and the constant need to summon courage[18] – perhaps like the woman of Gospel memory who with great determination sweeps her house.

Sixth, all of the above are only one side of the coin, as it were. For alongside Ann's emphasis on searching and courage is an emphatic belief that God searches in love for human persons. She would add to Evelyn Underhill's view that 'God extends an invitation to be loved to each and every human being',[19] that 'God does not leave human beings to flounder in their pains and difficulties but seeks them out'[20] – the invitation from the divine side is energetic, oriented towards the objects of God's love.

This brings us to the centre of Ann's convictions – divine grace. Unsurprisingly, then, 'grace' recurs as a keyword in what follows. It is clear that Ann believes that grace – kindness, beauty, generosity, loveliness and the cluster of good things this strange word enfolds – is *available* to human persons. But it is also evident that she thinks that this grace that is available is *empowering* of persons, able and meant to affect the way things are and could be, stirring up grit, agitating into life the mettle needed to change things for the better.

When Ann was installed as a canon of Durham Cathedral, Tom Wright, then bishop in that city, in his sermon for that occasion brought forward crucial characteristics of Ann and her work (and not only of her preaching). He framed his thoughts first in terms of Ann's ready willingness to voice a 'worrying prophecy': that is, to say what she sees going on in the world, name those left out, and articulate the associated challenges to Christians and churches, but also then to point towards a 'wonderful grace'. To quote Wright: 'part at least of what Ann Loades has been able under God, to facilitate [is]

---

18 'The practice of courage' is central to her view of spirituality; see Ann Loades, *Spiritual Classics from the Late Twentieth-century* (London: Church House Publishing, 1995), vi.

19 Loades, *Evelyn Underhill*, xii.

20 Loades, 'New Sense', 161.

the listening of the Church to the questions of the world, of the culture, the taking of those questions into the praying life of Christ in this place, and then return with fresh answers, a fresh word of grace'.

Grace is often paired – as it is in the title of this book – with 'glory', a word that Ann reminds her listeners means weight, authority, clout, and that is manifest when it gives power and 'passion for things to be different', as she puts it in another of her sermons. In Ann's understanding, such glory may be found by looking at human persons head on – in the face. And if Evelyn Underhill knew that it was not so much (or even much at all) what preachers say that is most important, but what others see and find in them – as Underhill put it, the 'atmosphere' they generate – it will be evident to those fortunate to know Ann Loades that this atmosphere is a quality she radiates. The texts of her sermons and addresses give us manifold and vivid glimpses: kindness and clout, grace and glory.

PART I

Mainly on the Lectionary

Preached between the early 1980s and late 2010s, and in a variety of contexts, the sermons here suggest the ways in which the term 'lectionary' is one that covers some flux: the Book of Common Prayer, for which there is clear affection in what follows; the Alternative Service Book *which was operative in the Church of England from 1980 to 1997; and from 1997,* Common Worship, *a variant of the ecumenical* Revised Common Lectionary *(RCL), itself close to the Roman Catholic lectionary for mass.* Common Worship, *for example, has sequences for principal, second and third services each Sunday. There is also a so-called 'pillar' lectionary, used in cathedrals, in which well-known and 'purple passages' of the Bible appear more frequently, geared to settings welcoming occasional worshippers likely to be unfamiliar with the range of more expansive reading schemes. A range of lectionaries were used across the occasions where these sermons were preached, though the note accompanying each one here relates Scripture portions to the RCL.*

I

Beginnings (Advent)

This is the time of the year when those who share in the worship of the Christian tradition begin to equip themselves for Advent – so, back to beginnings and the theme of creation for this morning's liturgy.[1] There's nothing simple about any of the texts chosen to illustrate the theme, but since beginnings is the theme, let us have another look at the first one in particular. What could be more familiar, and often used to foster exactly what we do not need nowadays, than hostility between human beings on the basis of their sexual-social identity. It may be with the greatest difficulty that we can clear our heads and imaginations of some of the interpretations this text has been made to bear throughout the centuries. As we all know, translation and interpretation easily run into one another, so the interests of the translator and interpreter and the hearers or readers have to be borne in mind. In our own time, we need to think very hard about the part 'religion' may play in fostering mistrust and hostility between one another and in the habitats we share with so many other creatures.

So, to Genesis, to 'beginnings'. If you know anything about the first couple of chapters you'll know that there are two stories about 'beginnings', with chapter 2 possibly older than chapter 1. Both celebrate life and delight in one another for the time in which we live. The story makes it clear that it is God's world as God shapes it, including rain, plants and herbs, and no one to till them – no 'Adam' yet, an earth creature, to serve God's earth. So God works like a potter, shaping the earth

---

1 Among the readings was Genesis 1.1—2.4a, a text found in the RCL not in Advent but for the Vigil of Easter, Years A, B and C.

creature from the dust, making it alive by breathing God's own breath into it. God then makes a garden in which to put this earth creature: a garden, 'Eden', a place of delight. The only thing we know about this earth creature so far is that it has nostrils, for God breathed into them. Given nostrils, the earth creature can enjoy the garden. Out of the very same earth from which the earth creature was made come trees and plants, so sight and taste are available as well! The garden bubbles with water, and so the earth creature can till it and keep it fertile with more or less responsible care. The word often translated as 'till' also means 'serve': we serve what we respect. So to keep the garden is not to possess it but to care for it and protect it. Responsible action is here service and caring protection, responsible to God, the potter, life-breather, garden planter; and now lawgiver. Eat this but not that. The earth creature can smell, breathe, taste, see, and hear these words – shaping up nicely, we might say, learning to live within limits. Eat the tree of the knowledge of good and evil, however, and it's not just big trouble, but death. Step out of the limits God sets for such a simple act as eating, and the results will not be life but the end of it.

God now goes in for a spot of job evaluation. It is not good for the earth creature to be alone, so more of the project develops, with a companion (someone to eat with). The word 'companion' is more usually translated as 'helper', but this is misleading in our society as it can so easily suggest an assistant, an inferior one at that. But in Hebrew it is used as a word for God, so if we take it with more of the phrase in which it is found, we find a 'partner', a 'companion' corresponding to the earth creature, built out of flesh, with God as matchmaker.

There is a major sorting out task to perform. For just as God made the earth creatures, they are to be found among God's animals and birds too (there are no fish in this story, even in those bubbling rivers!). They are identified as domestic animals, birds of the air, wild animals in this shared project with God who delegates the task to God's speaking creatures. For one and all, life is God-given, and the human sexual carnival is to be celebrated in another scripture, 'The Song of Songs'!

This is primarily a story about God, but is also an invitation to celebrate our world, to serve it, protect it, with all our senses at full stretch, with all the intelligence, imagination, sensitivity we can muster. We do indeed belong here, but we do not 'possess' it, as it is not 'ours'. For Christians, it is excellent preparation for the celebration of 'bone of my bone, flesh of my flesh' – the birth of Jesus of Nazareth from the body of his mother, which is another story about creation and beginnings and, mercifully for us, new beginnings, new possibilities: the gift of an infinitely ingenious God, fortunately for us.

2

Cana (Epiphany)

This is the season in which the Church reflects on various manifestations of Jesus of Nazareth as divine.[1] Suppose that around the turn of the first and second centuries of the Christian era there exists someone of exceptional insight sitting at a desk with an ample supply of writing materials to hand, thinking about how she or he too can make a contribution to understanding Jesus as a manifestation of the divine by writing a Gospel – a new literary form in response to an extraordinary series of events. Our author will certainly know about the suffering and death of Jesus, and of some strange encounters with Jesus after his death, and will know some of the traditions on which other Gospel writers drew – there were a number of other people, probably not known to one another, trying to get these traditions and memories into some sort of shape. How is our author going to make his own very distinctive version of what he knows?

In its finished form, he gave his book a unique kind of preface by way of introduction, using the simplest but most profound language, getting his hearers or readers familiar in just a few verses with some of the key terms he will explore further in his text: God, light, life, witness, world, flesh, grace, truth and glory. It is that last word, glory, we focus on in this morning's reading. But, and it is a big 'but', when we hear the word 'glory' we need to forget magnificence in all its forms, such as that which may be on display in a great state occasion, for example. Glory may indeed be manifest in the beauty and

---

1 Among the readings was John 2.1–11, appointed in the RCL for the Second Sunday of Epiphany, Year B.

splendour of God's creation, but it also has connotations of the weight of authority, authorization, clout, responsibility. So in Psalm 102.16 we find that 'the LORD will build up Zion, he will appear in his glory', but as we learn from this morning's Gospel, that appearance can be subtle, obscure except to a few, and eventually lead the one who manifests it to his death.

So let us stay with this morning's Gospel and what our author makes of divine glory in the person of Jesus of Nazareth. Unsurprisingly, he begins with John the Baptist, but instead of describing Jesus' baptism directly, we find John provoked into declaring Jesus as Spirit-bearer, and as the Lamb of God, the never-to-be-forgotten death of Jesus throughout the Gospel. Two of John's disciples attach themselves to Jesus, and Andrew ropes in Simon Peter; the pair of them find Philip, and they find Nathanael whose very name (most appropriately here!) means 'God gives' or 'God has given'. This is apt indeed for a man recognized by Jesus as being without guile, and who in turn acknowledges Jesus as being Son of God – the name in the Psalms used for the King of Israel and, as we know, dangerous to anyone for whom the claim is made. What then?

Here our author contributes something quite new to the Gospel tradition. He tells us that Nathanael comes from Cana, and indeed in his fidelity he turns up right at the end of the Gospel, at the breakfast party Jesus cooks for the disciples by the shore of the sea of Tiberias. From the point where Nathanael joins the group, we move straight to a wedding feast in Cana. Who knows, it might have been a member of Nathanael's family – what would be more natural than for him to take his new companions along? A marriage feast was one of the major occasions for festivity even in occupied territory, and we know from non-biblical sources that it would have involved a procession with the bridegroom's friends escorting the bride to her new home for festivities lasting about a week. Quite possibly not all the guests would arrive and stay at the same time – they might well bring their own tents and provisions and stay around the locality, as well as bringing contributions to the feast itself. Hospitality to them would include a good supply of clean water: to wash and soothe much-travelled feet, to clean and refresh head and face, to give a good final wash of arms and hands to make one presentable. The water would be found in the stone water jars at the host's home, as we find in the narrative of the marriage feast at Cana. They are just about empty when some of the guests arrive, and the servants have yet to refill them from the nearby well. And depending on how the calculations are done, those stone jars might between them hold between 120–150 gallons of water – more than enough to be going on with!

We know nothing about the family apart from the fact that they may have been related to Nathanael, but we do know about some of the guests. First of all, the mother of Jesus was present – one of only two occasions in this Gospel where she appears (the second being near the crucified one when he and a much-loved disciple are helped to commit themselves to one another to begin a new kind of family). Jesus' mother is not named as 'Mary' but is simply, as in the case of most other women in this Gospel, addressed as 'woman' – and we don't know how to take this, to be honest. Is it a formal and most courteous form of address? Even if it is, it's a bit odd in the words of a son to his mother. Or is it an indication of a certain distance between them – a hint of irritation even, pushing a little further away what is left of parental authority? Anyway, Jesus' mother is clearly a person of some standing in the gathering, as we see from the way she is to behave.

Jesus and his disciples are also invited to the marriage, and it is as though they have no sooner presented themselves than Jesus' mother informs him of what he would soon have discovered: much to the embarrassment of his host, 'they have no wine'. Something has gone wrong here. Of course, Jesus and his little group may have turned up without much to contribute to the celebration, but in any event he seems to have taken this information as a request for help. What is it that she knows about him that makes that credible? We are not told, but we may recall the scriptural blessings of the gifts of wine and oil, not least in association with the figure of divine wisdom. Does she think of him as in some sense the embodiment of that wisdom? We have no way of knowing. In response to 'they have no wine', however, Jesus' mother receives what seems like a brush-off. 'What have you to do with me?', but there's more to it than that. We know of other occasions in Scripture when the phrase is used, and it is usually on the lips of someone ill at ease, or stressed out, we might say (such as the widow whose son has died and who fears the effect of having the prophet Elijah on her premises, though in her case the prophet restores her son). We find the phrase elsewhere in the Gospels where demons challenge Jesus, who is going to destroy them and restore someone to sanity. But in this case it is Jesus who is using the phrase. It is he who is ill at ease, unsure of whether to act – 'my hour has not yet come' – but for what, if not for this? His mother's persistence pays off – there are other examples in the Gospels of persistence being effective at times too! – and she tells the servants to do whatever he tells them. What is at stake here for him? He simply tells the servants to fill up the stone water jars, but also to draw out the liquid and take it to the master of the feast. Was he just going to receive freshly drawn water? The servants, fortunately for them, know better, and so do his disciples. And our Gospel writer makes the point: this was the first of Jesus' 'signs' – what the other Gospels would call 'mighty works', but in this Gospel also including many other actions of Jesus. But the sign is not just 'first' in the sequence of what Jesus does, but first in the sense of 'primary' – it is for them the first trustworthy manifestation of his glory, his authority, his grace in response to a human need, his contribution to festivity, for all the privacy and obscurity of his words and actions here. And if our author has it right, it seems that the experience may have brought something into focus for Jesus himself. We find that our author goes on to write something equally extraordinary, but in a context anything but obscure. For when mother, brothers and disciples journey with Jesus to Capernaum, he leaves them and heads for Jerusalem, and it is here rather than much later in his Gospel that our author records the cleansing of the Temple, and the headlong controversy with Jesus about the status of the Temple that will be one of the things that will bring him to his death. Changing water into wine and the manifestation of divine authority in the obscurity of a wedding feast at Cana was one thing, but it seems to have precipitated Jesus into quite other and far more dangerous circumstances – as well he may of course have feared. But once he had agreed that his hour had indeed come, it would be Jerusalem and not Cana where divine glory would be manifested, with grim consequences for him as Lamb of God, as John the Baptist had foreseen.

3

Unclean

There's no time like the present.[1] Mark packs a lot into his first chapter – Jesus responding to the preaching of John the Baptist, finding himself in an opened heaven, Spirit-descending, hearing a divine voice, and as a direct consequence, we might say, Spirit-driven into the wilderness and beginning his conflict with Satan, God's adversary. John is quickly identified as a likely troublemaker, and imprisoned. Jesus will soon be identified as another, as Mark's Gospel tells us a couple of chapters later (Mark 3.6), and it also becomes clear that even his friends think he's problematic – 'beside himself', indeed, irresponsible (Mark 3.21). He spells trouble, and attention to him will mean attention to those who associate with him, which is the last thing they need. Galilee is a province governed by a son of Herod the Great, with Roman occupiers not too far away. It is a prosperous agricultural region, and no one wants agriculture, trade and travel disrupted by someone stirring up religious sensitivities. John is no sooner in prison – warning enough, one might think – than Jesus appears, wanting wholehearted commitment to God. Repent, trust God, and take risks to show commitment to the conviction that God indeed does reign – Herod's son and the Romans are not unlimitedly important. And it's all very well summoning those first followers from their trade of fishing, something that cannot have made him exactly popular with their families, dependent as they would be on their skills and energies. Safety in numbers? What now? There is no time like the present, so off they go to Capernaum, and into the synagogue on the sabbath.

1 A reading was Mark 1.21–28, appointed in the RCL for the Third Sunday after the Epiphany, Year B.

11

We know a bit about synagogues as houses of prayer, places for community gatherings, with schooling on offer for boys from a very young age who would learn their letters, read and chant texts out loud. They would learn an extraordinary amount by heart, becoming what in later Judaism were known as 'living texts', even being capable of expounding the texts. Jesus presumably went to synagogue school in Nazareth. Closely connected with each synagogue were a group of scribes, lawyers rather like today's solicitors, responsible for contracts and settlements, and for teaching the boys. Their job was to transmit tradition, and as when the principal person in a synagogue invited someone to speak, the expectation would be that the invited person would comment on the text that had been read, and what he said would be recognizable as part and parcel of tradition. On this particular occasion of Jesus' joining the Capernaum synagogue for prayers, those present are in for something of a shock. 'He taught them as one who had authority, and not as the scribes.' It is possible that this means that he simply ignored the readings for that particular sabbath, and taught them to repent, to trust God and to take risks, to show their conviction that God does indeed reign, and in such a way that they recognized that they were in the presence of someone exceptional. Recall the words from our first reading, from Deuteronomy 18.18, words supposedly addressed to no less a person than Moses: 'I will raise up for them a prophet like you from among their brethren; and I will put my words in his mouth, and he shall speak to them all that I command him.' Are they confronted by a prophet in the person of Jesus? We know that he was a teacher of great originality, and Mark gives us six main examples of Jesus' parables. Maybe one of them was tried out on this occasion. Anyway, Jesus simply does not belong to any recognized group of scribes in the way he goes about things. He draws on his memorized inheritance, makes it very much his own and shapes it afresh for his hearers. It does not, of course, follow that everyone was enthusiastic about what he said or how he said it. Amazed they certainly were, and questioning. So far, more or less so good, we might say, but in the synagogue in Capernaum that day there was more and indeed worse to come.

For in the synagogue was a man 'with an unclean spirit' – 'unclean' meaning something like 'out of place', or 'not wanted until cleaned up', as though some of that satanic conflict from the wilderness had somehow sneaked itself into the synagogue to cause trouble. And this man, being in a way 'inspired' by that 'unclean spirit', voices some of the fears of the congregation: 'What have you to do with us, Jesus of Nazareth? Have you come to destroy us? I know who you are, the Holy One of God.' Jesus rebukes him, tells him to hold his peace, and commands the 'unclean spirit' to come out of the man. Now, we know something of how a young boy learned the Jewish tradition of his day. We have no idea of how someone discovered that they had the kind of authority that Jesus here displays over this 'unclean spirit'. How did Jesus come to know that he had this kind of authority? Was it a discovery from his experience of baptism, put to some sort of test in the confrontation with Satan in the wilderness, with the first moment of its public exercise in the synagogue? Or was this occasion in the synagogue the moment of discovery? Jesus was identified, and feared. Maybe it was not the last occasion on which Jesus discovered something about himself that was almost forced out of him in a head-on conflict, as a kind of gift to him. And the conclusion of the narrative in Mark is the recognition of Jesus' authority in both teaching and in his capacity to make the 'unclean' obey him: that is to say, to make them 'clean', in place back in the community. But the incident exacts its price, for Jesus can hardly escape from the many who need his help, not least help in release from inexplicable evils, health by exorcism. It is no accident that one of his most characteristic habits was to get away completely on his own for considerable periods of time to rest and to pray (Mark 3.35).

The problem in reading Mark's Gospel, as so many commentators indicate, is that we might just be able to swallow Jesus the teacher, or even Jesus the healer. Some human beings do indeed seem to have extraordinary gifts almost inconceivable to most of us, and possibly thoroughly unwelcome if we found we possessed them. The rub comes with some of the miracles, and among them the exorcisms. Six parables in Mark, but miracle after miracle after miracle. We cannot dodge the problem, for the crowd in Capernaum link teaching and exorcism together as manifestation of the same authority. 'What is this? A new teaching! With authority he commands even the unclean spirits, and they obey him.' We cannot get away with Jesus the teacher and healer minus the exorcisms.

The problem of how to think of Jesus as teacher, healer and exorcist remains. Some commentators inform us that people in Jesus' day thought of what we now refer to as forms of derangement or madness as possession by 'unclean spirits' or demons, the implication being that we in our enlightened days know better – better than Jesus did, if it comes to that. We cannot deal this morning with every problem about how to think about Jesus of Nazareth but I suggest we can make some headway on what might be meant by 'unclean spirits' for our time. We can get some illumination here from a short story by the American writer Flannery O'Connor. I suggest that she may have taken this incident in the synagogue in Capernaum to heart, thereby shedding some light on what 'unclean spirit' might mean for us. The story is called 'Revelation', and to begin with one may well be puzzled by the title. For here in a doctor's waiting room are Mrs Turpin and her husband and it quickly becomes clear how Mrs Turpin values herself. O'Connor builds up her character very carefully. Here is one brief indication of what Mrs Turpin is like. She lists the classes of people to keep herself amused. 'On the bottom of the heap were most colored people, not the kind she would have been if she had been one, but most of them.' Next were 'white trash'. Just above them, home owners. Above the home owners, 'home-and-land owners' – the level at which she ranked herself. O'Connor continues: 'Usually by the time she had fallen asleep all the classes of people were moiling and roiling around in her head, and she would dream that they were all crammed together in a box car, being ridden off to be put in a gas oven.'[2]

---

2 See Flannery O'Connor, 'Revelation', in her collection, *Everything that Rises Must Converge* (London: Faber, 1987), 191–218.

Also present in the doctor's waiting room is a fat, ugly, acne-ridden, clever, college-age young woman who had become all too aware of Mrs Turpin and her opinions, liberally proclaimed to those in the waiting room with her whether they want to listen to her or not. This young woman suddenly throws her book at Mrs Turpin, and it hits her in the face; she then hurls herself across the room and sinks her fingers into Mrs Turpin's neck. The young woman seems to be having some kind of seizure. When the pair of them are separated, and Mrs Turpin has regained her power of motion, she demands that the girl speak, and waits, 'as for a revelation'. When the girl raises her head, her gaze locks with Mrs Turpin's and the girl whispers up to her, 'Go back to hell where you came from, you old wart hog.'

After this shocking encounter, back home and in the evening, Mrs Turpin takes over the hosing down of her pigs and grumbles over her day. Mercifully, despite her awfulness, she is not completely without perception, for who is she addressing in her fury? 'Who do you think you are?' she roars out at the pasture. And Mrs Turpin is given a most extraordinary response. First, everything she sees is 'burned for a moment with a transparent intensity'. When she tries to open her mouth, no sounds come forth. And then what she sees is a streak of purple cutting through the crimson of the sky, a streak that she sees 'as a vast swinging bridge extending upwards ... Upon it a vast horde of souls were rumbling toward heaven', including all the people she had so despised and would be happy to see dead, with those at the end being people like herself, and her husband, though they look shocked and noticeably different. She is much blessed, made clean, we could say, for as she turns for home she can hear 'the voices of the souls climbing upward into the starry field and shouting hallelujah'.

The point of this is to get us over thinking that talk of 'unclean spirits' can have no meaning for us, part and parcel of a worldview we no longer share. I doubt if it's that simple. Whatever else we know about human beings, we know that like Mrs Turpin we can be gripped and driven by terrible fears – some of them justified and some of them deep and irrational prejudices. Almost certainly we are not as nice as we might think we are in our worst moment of self-flattery, and the truth is that given half a chance, we are unclean spirits to someone or other. The remedy is clear enough, however, as in that synagogue in Capernaum: repent, trust God, take risks for the kingdom, especially taking the risk of paying attention to those who can help us clean ourselves up. We need to pray to God that they do it gently; above all, we must pray that we in our turn learn to be gentle with one another, without the shocking sort of confrontation so painful for poor Mrs Turpin.

4

Exodus (on the Transfiguration)

Since we are nowhere near the feast of the Transfiguration in early August, we may very well wonder why we have this morning's readings.[1] We could, of course, reflect in detail on the narrative, and we do indeed need to undertake some of that task before focusing in on just one word in the narrative. So, what do we need to bear in mind?

Notice to begin with that the reading came from St Luke's Gospel, although the Transfiguration is narrated in all of the first three Gospels, and the point of it suffuses the fourth Gospel. What has led up to this particular, Lucan version? And what do we need to recall when we read this chunk of Luke's words? We need to bear in mind that Luke has made it clear that Jesus will inevitably be on a collision course with the major authorities of his day. Recall that Gabriel has informed Mary that her son 'will be great and will be called the Son of the Most High', given David's throne and reign for ever. Mary's own song of praise is full of confidence that God will scatter the proud and bring down rulers. Zechariah promises that God gives salvation from enemies and from the hand of the haters – whoever they are. An angel informs shepherds that the baby they are invited to see is both Saviour and Lord – titles used for emperors – and that his reign is to be one of peace. And they all live, we recall, in occupied territory in which they can trust neither Romans nor client-kings nor religious authorities, all

---

1 The readings included Luke 9.28–36, appointed for the Last Sunday after the Epiphany, Year C. The Feast of the Transfiguration itself is 6 August.

of whom cooperate with one another to maintain some sort of order. Those who disturb that order are given short shrift.

When Jesus begins his ministry, he takes these promises upon himself. He announces that he is endowed with the Spirit of God, anointed to preach deliverance. He deliberately gathers around him the nucleus of a new social group, and demonstrates his own extraordinary power in the healings of the sick and possessed. Most terrifying of all, as in this present reading, he is astonishingly close to God. He prays on a mountain and two of the great figures of Israel's past appear with him: first, Moses, whose face had glistened on Sinai when he conversed with God, and whose burial place was strangely unknown (by Jesus' time, he was believed to have been caught up into heaven), and second, Elijah, whose confrontational life was believed to have ended with him being caught up in a chariot to heaven. Both Moses and Elijah mediated God's glory to Israel, and the reflected light on Moses' face was an indication of that glory. The word 'glory' means more than light, radiance and beauty; it includes weight, clout, authority, presence. Moses and Elijah appear in glory, in a transformed state indeed, but as authoritative presences, mediating divine presence and authority. And if there was any doubt about whether Jesus should be in their company, divine speech comes from the cloud that veils the overwhelming splendour of God: 'This is my Son, my chosen, listen to him.'

So what is to be the main topic of the exchange between Moses, Elijah and Christ?

Here is the response to the question with which we began: this is not the feast of the Transfiguration, so why this reading? It is masked in the translation as 'speaking of his departure'. The word is 'exodus'. 'Departure' is a poor translation for a word signifying an act of divine deliverance, the fulfilment of all those promises. And the only certainty is that it won't look like anything of the kind. Being on the receiving end of a particularly gruesome form of a death penalty does not encourage anyone to see Jesus as the one who manifests in his own person divine authority, as divine beauty. Ah well, we might say, we know what the gospel claims, that by the time we get to Easter we will have been reassured, and so we can go on much as before and, at one level, thank God that is true. Most of us in our time will not have to face anything so terrible.

But let us relate Jesus' 'exodus' to the life and death of someone rather closer to our own time than the 'Jesus of history' – not that it is appropriate to think of Jesus in that way if we believe the 'exodus', deliverance theme of Luke's Gospel. Yesterday in the Church's calendar we recalled the life and death of Janani Luwum, Archbishop of Uganda, one of the twentieth century's many martyrs. For some, Jesus' exodus may represent an awesome summons to do what Jesus did – that is, put oneself on a collision course with a brutal and uncompromising authority. Luwum was born in 1922, and spent part of his young life as a goatherd. He was fortunate in one sense, for given half a chance at school he was remarkably intelligent, quick to learn, and he later qualified as a teacher. On 6 January 1948 he experienced a conversion, roughly at midday! He was sent to the London College of Divinity for further study. To a great extent he was the product of colonial and imperialist culture, but back in Uganda, perhaps unsurprisingly, he began to think very hard about how to shift the gospel into his own context. With increasing responsibility, first as Bishop of Northern Uganda from 1969, then as Archbishop of Uganda from 1974, he learned not only to cooperate with his Roman Catholic colleagues (something that could not have been expected of him in his young days) but to dig his heels in against the appalling regime of Idi Amin, responsible in one way or another for the deaths of some 300,000 Ugandans between 1971 and 1978. Luwum's conversations with his fellow bishops reinforced their protests at what had become a policy of state-instigated mass murder. Luwum and two government ministers were killed in a car crash, planned on presidential instructions, on 17 February 1977. It was the same year, incidentally, in which Steve Biko was killed by white security forces in South Africa – just to remind ourselves that no culture or country, least of all our own, has a monopoly on brutality or wickedness.

Nothing to do with us, we may think, thank God – but

you never know. Neither Jesus in Nazareth nor Luwum in his days as a goatherd could possibly have foreseen where fidelity to God might take them, and we may well pray to be spared such appalling possibilities. Our own forms of fidelity may be obscure, minor by comparison, less costly, less demanding. We are not so courageous, thoughtful, perceptive – but you never know. In the meantime, keep Janani Luwum and others of his like in mind when we participate in the exodus meal of the Eucharist, understood at the very least as the celebration of the deliverance that Moses, Elijah and Jesus spoke about on the Mount of the Transfiguration.

5

Saying No (Lent)

We find ourselves at the beginning of the time of year when up here in Northern Europe the days begin to lengthen.[1] In gratitude we welcome the light and sunshine that has begun to reappear, with all the promise it brings of spring, of the change of seasons, of new beginnings, marked by the flowers and birds and other small creatures more evident in our gardens. The word 'Lent' has come to be virtually a synonym for 'spring', and the returning light shows us things in a new way, highlighting the occasional cobweb, dusty corner or bleary window. Sooner or later we have to engage in spring-cleaning and spring-sorting, and by tradition the Church calendar nudges us into beginning early enough, with Lent – a good stretch before Easter – making it possible to ready things for another time of celebration.

So this is a good time of year to sort out and dispose of the clutter of our lives: the clothes we don't wear, the household items we don't use, the books we won't read again, the music we won't play again. All those things can be turned over to agencies who will see to it that they reach those who simply do not have anything to give away, or who can sell the things we neither want nor need and use the cash for things others immediately need – food and clothing for starters. Our living spaces, and we ourselves, may thankfully be so much more pleasant if we are somewhat less burdened, with less to bother about, if we travel lighter! There are many unobtrusive ways of practising generosity to those less showered with wholly undeserved

---

1 A reading was Isaiah 58.1–12, appointed for Ash Wednesday in Years A, B and C of the RCL.

blessings than we are, and we don't need to make any kind of song or dance about it. Just do it. Every single one of us can do something, however small it seems, to make a bit of a difference to someone else who deserves a share of the blessings at least as much as we do. We all share much the same kind of life, and have much the same needs. It is rarely the fault of the most vulnerable if they sometimes fall on very hard times, but it is our fault if they do not receive some help because we are mean with ourselves and what we own.

Every small act of generosity pushes back the boundaries of the covetousness, the avarice, the seductions of 'must have' that are presented to us almost wherever we look. To fall for avarice is to turn us into greedy guzzlers, not least of food. Think back to the Tuesday before Lent, Mardi Gras in some parts of the world, 'Fat Tuesday' – the day for eating lots of goodies, a day that was meant to mark the point at which we would *not* eat delectable goodies again for a stretch of time. In some places that day would be the last of the winter carnival, cheerfully getting into the mood in which we learn again to live without the food of the rich, whatever that food is for us. The stretch of time ahead is by tradition 40 days, which is why the first Sunday in Lent used to be known as Quadrigesima – the Latin for the Greek meaning the fortieth day back from Easter.

Forty days is about a tenth of the year, so we might think about it as a kind of tithe of our time, long enough for a bit of cheerful austerity, long enough to promote a new habit, giving it a little more time to take hold. It's not easy, of course, in a society where supermarkets stock strawberries and red roses and so many other out-of-season delights. A bit of austerity means a little more cash freed up for charities, of which there are many to choose in all conscience. So, think Isaiah 58.6–7:

Is not this the fast that I choose:
to loose the bonds of wickedness,
to undo the thongs of the yoke,
to let the oppressed go free,
and to break every yoke?
Is it not to share your bread with the hungry,

and to bring the homeless poor into your house;
when you see the naked, to cover him,
and not to hide yourself from your own flesh?

We can give things up to be freed up ourselves and free others up a bit. But charity apart, there's another reason why fasting matters: and the reason is that we need to practise saying 'no' to the good so that we can say 'no' to the bad, which may be amazingly attractive. The point is that as and when (not if and when) we are faced with situations in which we simply must not collude, turn a blind eye, stand aside, obey orders or fall in with a suggestion that we abuse whatever power we have, we will already, graced by God, have got ourselves into training, be mature enough to say 'no'. We need to become the kinds of people who just will not bully or abuse the vulnerable, the frail, the young, the poor, the captives, those junior to us at work. If we can't learn to say 'no' to the things we most enjoy, and quite rightly too at times of celebration, we will never become mature enough to say 'no' when a crunch comes, which it very possibly will, somewhere along the line.

It is no accident that the Gospels tell us not only of Christ's first 40 days in the wilderness but of his habit of regularly backing off into deserted places, or up mountainsides. Of course he needed times when he was free from the demands of others, but he needed also to shake himself free of the seductions on offer, so that he could say 'no' to them and 'yes' to God. Hear Isaiah again, and think of it as true of Christ, of the man so given to care about others:

Then shall your light break forth like the dawn,
and your healing shall spring up speedily;
your righteousness shall go before you,
the glory of the LORD shall be your rear guard.
Then you shall call, and the LORD will answer;
you shall cry, and he will say, Here I am. (Isaiah 58.8–9)

There, if you like, is a portrait of Christ, a man open to the presence of God because he has learned so thoroughly what to resist and what to embrace; what to reject and what to love. And it would not have been achieved in just one stretch in the desert, but repeatedly recovered and renewed as he lived the vocation that brought him both to death and also to a re-created, God-given life now shared with us. So for us, Lent, every year, is a chance to get a little bit further on with being a little more Christ-like, a little more open to God.

And that is why at this time we are invited to line up with candidates preparing for baptism at Easter. They undergo a sort of spring-cleaning of themselves in preparation for joining up with Christ in his practice of the presence of God, leading to his death but also to his resurrection. It is a good time for those already baptized to support candidates for baptism, praying for them, renewing life together. Shrove Tuesday was the day for being 'shriven', shedding whatever holds us back, getting ourselves turned around, refocused, reoriented. By the time Easter comes, we may be a little bit thinner, a little bit poorer, a little bit braver, more hopeful, more determined, a little happier – all in all, in better shape to celebrate Easter than last year. Recall Isaiah once more, but this time as a possibility even for ourselves: 'You shall call, and the Lord will answer; you shall cry, and he will say, Here I am.'

6

Justice and Only Justice

I remember vividly the experience of learning to drive – not so much becoming responsible for myself in a new way, driving a vehicle, but rather suddenly becoming aware for the first time in my life of being a pedestrian, of what it meant to be on my feet.[1] As a pedestrian, I was obviously a complete menace – not alert, not looking, but expecting other people to be aware of where I was and what I was doing; expecting cars to be able to brake at any distance! I'm not even sure I was particularly alert to *other* people on *their* feet, come to think about it. I simply hadn't made the connections between myself and others that I needed to make.

I'm ashamed to say that I've recently had a similar sort of experience in relation to liturgy. In some ways I'd been behaving like the pedestrian I was before I learned to drive. Of course, I'd been physically present at liturgies of one sort or another for years. I'd turned up, sat, knelt and stood, used my ears to listen, my voice to sing, seen the symbols, received bread or wafers into my hands, tasted the wine. I'd been there, done all that, often enough. And, in theory, I could have said some of the right things about how liturgy and life experience flow out and in from one another, across, through and around whatever boundaries we set, rather desperately, to keep them apart. After all, it wouldn't do to take the connections too seriously, would it? We'd have to cope with change – in ourselves, in our institutions, the way we go about things, how we plan. We throw up the barricades all right, but liturgy and living keep pushing them over – or so I'd have said.

---

1 A reading was Isaiah 58.1–12, always appointed in the RCL for Ash Wednesday.

So what turned me into a different sort of liturgical pedestrian – or at least may be turning me into one? Partly, I admit, the experience of the rough equivalent of some introductory driving lessons – their liturgical equivalent. Giving the occasional sermon; learning to teach others what's going on in liturgy and sacrament; thinking philosophically about the integrity of word and action; being licensed to do the awesome task of administering the chalice at Holy Communion. In a way, none of that should have been necessary, any more than I should have had to learn to drive to learn to be a responsible pedestrian.

Beyond all that, though, part of what has been happening – I hope – has at long last been the sheer impact of the liturgy itself, in which like beginners in music playing scales and arpeggios we repeat and repeat God's action on our behalf. Perhaps it's begun to sink in – incarnation, body, blood, bread, water, fire, wine, death and resurrection; praise, gratitude, petition, confession, repentance, service, blessing, grace, glory; all that stuff about salt in food, light in darkness, yeast in bread – such simple images, so profound. And the inescapable note of judgement – *you* saw it, *you* were there. What did *you* say, what did *you* do? Are you blind, deaf, without a voice?

Some of the texts must have impinged at long last, made their marks in my imagination, in the way I see the world differently, as I become a different sort of liturgical pedestrian. It's Lent, so what about this text?

Is not this the fast that I choose:
to loose the bonds of wickedness,
to undo the thongs of the yoke,
to let the oppressed go free,
and to break every yoke?
Is it not to share your bread with the hungry,
and bring the homeless poor into your house;
when you see the naked, to cover him,
and not to hide yourself from your own flesh?
Then shall your light break forth like the dawn,
and your healing shall spring up speedily;

your righteousness shall go before you,
the glory of the LORD shall be your rear guard.
Then you shall call, and the LORD will answer,
you shall cry, and he will say, Here I am. (Isaiah 58.6–9)

Jesus of Nazareth would have learned these words as a boy,
so it's not in the least surprising that we find him teaching that
those who hunger and thirst after such righteousness will be
blessed, and find fulfilment, or that he behaves like a slave,
doing for his disciples what a woman had done for him, washing their feet. On one occasion he turns up at a synagogue
liturgy and reads another text from Isaiah:

> The Spirit of the Lord is upon me, because he has anointed
> me to preach good news to the poor. He has sent me to pro-
> claim release to the captives and recovering of sight to the
> blind, to set at liberty those who are oppressed, to proclaim
> the acceptable year of the Lord. (Luke 4.18–19)

God's initiative, yes, but his feet, his voice, his commitment to
justice – something he learned in the heart of liturgy itself. So:
close the gap between the promise of the text and its realization;
and be brief, blunt and to the point, not as a matter of 'charity'
(important though that may be as a temporary palliative, if
it can be offered in the right kind of way and not add insult
to injury already inflicted) but as a matter of the justice God
requires. Take Jesus' prayer: 'Thy kingdom come' is a political
text if ever there was one. Whose world is it anyway? Again
according to Isaiah, the whole world is full of God's glory,
God's authority, like it or not, go with it or against it. And
political means personal – it's about face-to-face interaction,
where we live, where we are, not just political in the sense
of relatively impersonal big-scale policymaking, crucial and
important as we know it to be. Return to Isaiah: 'Not to hide
yourself from your own flesh' – is that what we do, at all levels:
literally turn our backs on one another, refuse the face-to-face,
not seeing, not talking, and above all not listening? And think
again: liturgy includes intercession, petition. Not that God

needs to be informed of what we want or need, but God needs to know that we know we need it, that we really do passionately *want* it:

> Then you shall call, and the LORD will answer;
> you shall cry, and he will say, Here I am.

Petition is, at least in part, protest. Martha confronted Jesus: 'If you had been here, my brother would not have died.' Mary confronted a man she thought was a gardener: what have they done with him, where is he? The protest, the tears – so the brother restored, Christ restored to those who loved him enough to protest, enough to cry. If we don't mind enough, nothing will happen, because nothing can happen without the anguish and indeed the anger that is released in protest, in the passion for things to be different.

Of course it's inescapably mucky stuff: guilt, conflict, compromise, alienation, screwing it up, dead ends, getting it appallingly wrong – but that, surely, isn't what God finds disgusting in the pursuit of justice. After all, it's transformation all the way: bread out of wheat, wine out of grapes, life out of death, a body made glorious because of its scars, not in spite of them; forgiveness – new beginnings. What's disgusting, rather, is not putting intelligence, imagination, determination, courage, the flair of the entrepreneur, the willingness to take risks, to act generously, *at God's disposal*, so that homes, offices, factories, schools, businesses, streets, pubs, clubs and fun are all graced by justice. So: 'the glory of the Lord shall be your rearguard'. What else could we need?

To focus on liturgy again – what, after all, does the word mean? People and work, work and people, work of the people; or more neatly, amazingly, public service, public services. Perhaps the Church will be one of the places where we might again discover and rediscover what that phrase could mean. And attendance seems to be commanded. Do it, he said. Turning up isn't optional. Think how maddening it is when someone doesn't turn up for rehearsals, for planning and policy meetings, let alone when they absent themselves from the play itself, from the decisions, the rewriting, the practice of commitment, from the commitment itself. And Holy Communion is, in Greek, *koinonia hagion* – the making common of the holy, sanctifying, the common, getting the two together, thinking of them not as something apart but interacting with each other. Recall too that the word 'mass' comes from the *last* phrase of the eucharistic liturgy: *ite, missa est*. You've had rations for the journey, a drink for the road, you've had your feet washed, so out, off you go. 'Go in peace to love and serve the Lord', says the liturgy; but better, I think, is Augustine's 'Sing Alleluia – and keep on walking'!

7

Mercy

For once, all four scriptural texts this morning clearly relate to a common theme: that of turning to God.[1] The text from Isaiah 55 is from the last chapter of the second section of Isaiah. It is the 'last words', as it were, from the poet-prophet of the time of exile, a time in which at least one thing has been learned. God seeks his people and they can seek God, wherever they are. God offers an invitation to life, to feasting, to the drinking of wine, water and milk, to a renewed covenant. And this is a gift to everyone. It is no longer primarily a gift to a king – who no longer exists, and never will exist for them again in the old way – but a gift to a particular community, to share with others. Incline your ear, come, seek, call, return, for God will have mercy, abundantly pardon, beyond our ability to imagine. That conviction that God is revealed as mercy goes right back to the desert experience of Moses at the burning bush, and remains a theme of central importance.

It is as though the writer of Psalm 63 responds to that invitation of Isaiah. The psalmist thirsts for God, and seems to have taken some rug or mat into the restored sanctuary in Jerusalem to stay overnight, waiting for the break of dawn in all its beauty, the light that will show him something of the divine strength and loving-kindness. The writer recalls earlier trust in God, praising God, praying with uplifted hands. And joining a feast again is the best metaphor for recovering trust in God.

Both of these texts would have been familiar to Jesus of Nazareth and to at least some of his followers. When we find him in Luke 13, partway along the grim journey to Jerusalem

---

1 The Gospel was Luke 13.1–9, appointed for the Third Sunday in Lent in the RCL, Year C.

by way of Galilee and Samaria and Jericho, Jesus can presume a lot in his stern warnings. God is indeed mercy, but is a judge too.

So far as the incidents included in this bit of Luke are concerned, because they are found nowhere else in any of the Gospels we have no idea of them apart from this text. Would even Pilate have authorized the slaughter of men at worship? The building accident is perhaps more believable. Either way, the point is clear. There is no necessary connection between such disasters and being turned away from God; nor will trust in God inevitably mean protection from disaster. What matters is a relationship to God, and it is being out of such a relationship that's the real disaster. Do Jesus' hearers believe that the most important thing at stake is trust in and fidelity to God no matter what? God's abundant mercy means that they can bear fruit, as the parable urges, rather than be like the kind of tree that's good for nothing except to make way for something better. There's a lot more to be said on this theme in Luke's Gospel, of course, such as the parables that conclude with the words about joy in heaven over even just one person who turns to God, but if they do, they are expected to live in certain ways.

And here Jesus parts company with the writer of Psalm 63. For the bit we didn't hear is concerned with the fate of the psalmist's opponents: 'They shall be given over to the power of the sword, they shall be prey for jackals' (verse 10). There's plenty of this in the Psalms, and nowadays we don't like to hold up a mirror to our own faces by saying or singing such words – words that often express what we really feel about those who differ from us or who do us down in some way, as we in turn do to them. We need safe places and safe times to say and sing such things, remembering that we are someone else's opponent, and they would like to see us put to the sword, as it were. We must get beyond thinking and speaking of one another in that way, but if we need to say and sing such things, remember always that human justice is a necessary but somewhat frail representation of the justice that is God's. Jesus clearly expects more of those who trust God – that they love even their enemies and do good to those who hate them. 'Be merciful, even as your Father is merciful' (Luke 6.36). So if we want to know what sort of fruit to bear, there's some tough work on ourselves ahead, tough and risky, and sometimes very problematic in our troubled societies, because mercy does not and cannot mean simply accepting everything that happens or everything we do.

Paul, in a letter to the Corinthians, picks this problem up. It is not the case that we can turn to God and think we can carry on much as before. Think of your predecessors in the desert, Paul suggests to his hearers. They too were given signs of divine presence – a baptism, a meal – and Christ was given to them in the desert but because of the way they behaved, God to them was judge. He cut them down, as the parable promises to those who do not bear fruit. And there is a special word of caution to those who think they can rely on themselves under stress. 'Therefore let any one who thinks that he stands take heed lest he fall' (1 Cor. 10.12). Think of Peter in Luke's Gospel (22.33), so disastrously insisting that he is ready to go with Jesus to prison and to death: Jesus tries to get across to him that it is God's fidelity to Peter that will sustain him in the end, no matter what. And then? That terrible moment in the fire-lit courtyard when Peter does indeed deny knowledge of Jesus, and Jesus turns and looks at him. Peter goes out and weeps bitterly at that look of love. No wonder then that Paul insists that it is God's fidelity to us that will make it possible to withstand whatever befalls us. And we might add, whether we explicitly know it, or not.

Let me conclude by giving you one example that I think makes this point. Hans Fallada's novel *Alone in Berlin*,[2] written after the fall of Germany in 1946–7, was the work of a man who was himself deeply troubled, but who nevertheless found a way to honour the risk-taking of decent citizens in the midst of horror. Fallada wrote in fictional form of the real-life resistance of a couple, Otto and Elise Hampel, who had undertaken a three-year campaign against the regime that was bringing about so much suffering. They took to leaving postcards all

---

2 Hans Fallada, *Alone in Berlin* (London: Melville House, 1947), with subsequent references noted in the main text.

over Berlin, calling for civil disobedience and workplace sabotage. They particularly urged citizens not to give to the Winter Fund, which was supposed to make possible charitable distribution to the needy but was in fact funding the war in which so many were dying and those who lived were being turned into criminal killers. Systematic and careful police work and some accidental slips eventually identified the couple, who were tried, sentenced and executed in 1943. Fallada had mental health and addiction problems and barely survived the war. A government minister in Eastern Germany handed him the police file on the Hampels and suggested he write about them. Fallada wrote the novel in just 24 days. It is unsurprising that Fallada seems to have been a little uncertain about how to express his conviction of the importance of the Hampels' fundamental human decency. We may well say that they were the wheat among the tares, to use a metaphor from a parable. Particularly moving is the exchange between Otto and the police inspector who would take credit for his capture. The inspector asks him what on earth he had hoped to accomplish – like a gnat against an elephant. Otto replies, 'You see, it doesn't matter if one man fights or ten thousand; if the man sees he has no option but to fight then he will fight, whether he has others on his side or not. I had to fight and given the choice I would do it again. Only I would do it very differently' (p. 417).

The inspector finds that he cannot withstand Otto, who says to him, 'You're working in the employ of a murderer, delivering ever new victims to him' (p. 418). Otto proposes that the inspector does it for money without sharing the conviction of his gruesome employer. At midnight, in his office, recognizing the truth of what his prisoner has said, the inspector kills himself in despair. Eventually, Otto dies with as much dignity as he can muster. The last words of the novel are about reaping what we have sown, and it is clear enough what the author thinks about the ultimate significance of such protest as the dissidents have been able to marshal. They are understood at the throne of God.

My point is to provide an example of what Paul could mean

by God's fidelity to us making it possible for us to withstand whatever befalls us, whether we explicitly know it or not. Otto and his wife display their decency in their dissidence in a terrible society, and Otto in his way turns to God as best he can, though it is others who explicitly believe in God, not he himself. And even the desperate inspector, challenged by and acknowledging the truth of what Otto has said to him, makes his own turn to God, and we may believe he is also embraced by the divine mercy.

I think one could not be an Otto unless one is in the habit of practising small acts of decency – indications, however small, of the turn to God of which Isaiah and the psalmist speak, and Jesus of Nazareth urges on his followers. And our austerities in Lent, large or small, are fundamentally about us making and sustaining that turn to God: a bit of toughening up so that in reliance on God we may become more like the fig tree that bears fruit rather than the fig tree that can only be uprooted, good for nothing at the end of the day.

8

A Pinch of Salt

This morning's reading is taken from a section of St Luke's Gospel concerned with training in discipleship.[1] In reading it we need to recall some features of Luke's portrayal of Jesus so far. Already in his Gospel Luke has made it clear that Jesus will inevitably be on a collision course with the authorities of his day. Gabriel tells Mary that her son will be 'the Son of the Most High', given David's throne and reign for ever. Mary's Magnificat promises that God will scatter the proud and bring down rulers. Zechariah announces that God gives salvation from enemies and from the hand of the haters. An angel speaks to shepherds to tell them the baby they are invited to see as both Saviour and Lord, one whose reign is to be of peace. All these persons live, we remember, in occupied territory, in a context of much distrust. It is a situation in which authorities have the responsibility of cooperating with one another to maintain some sort of public order, and in which disturbances of that order were liable to be met with harshness.

When Jesus emerges in Galilee and begins what we so blandly refer to as his ministry, rather than his confrontation of these authorities, he takes these promises upon himself. In Luke 4 he announces that he is endowed with the Spirit of God, anointed to preach deliverance. He deliberately gathers round him the nucleus of a new social group. How kindly we have been treated this morning in being spared the reading of Luke 14.26 – that discomfiting piece of hyperbole about hating

---

1 A reading was Luke 14.25–33, appointed for the Sunday between 4 and 10 September inclusive in Year C of the RCL (the occasion of the sermon was Lent 2, Year C, for which the *Common Worship* lectionary for the second service has Luke 14.27–33).

father, mother, wife, even children, brethren and sisters – 'yea, even one's own life' – as necessary for discipleship. Those who select our readings perhaps wanted to spare congregations yet another sermon about Jesus' words not really meaning what they appear to say – and I've already softened them by speaking of them as hyperbole. But there is a sort of ruthlessness about them, and we are hardly spared their implications since our reading pitches into Jesus' words about cross-bearing, with a later verse speaking of the need to forsake all that we have. Jesus is not exactly the sort of person we easily associate with commitment to family connections, at least not when the demands of the kingdom as he sees them are put in front of possible disciples.

Luke has also recounted the extraordinary scene of the Transfiguration, in which Jesus has conversed with Moses and Elijah about the exodus deliverance he is to accomplish in Jerusalem, and a divine voice has again confirmed him as God's Son, his chosen one, with the injunction to listen to him. He terrifies his disciples by steadfastly setting his face towards Jerusalem, and embarks on the sort of instructions we find in this morning's readings. At this point, we can of course cheer ourselves up by thinking of our charitable giving as a small sign of sacrifice in the interests of others of God's creatures, or whatever else we do to flatter ourselves through Lent, as we look forward to Easter; and once past Easter Day perhaps carry on much as before.

But suppose we reflect on these words and take them with utter seriousness, at least to the extent of keeping in mind those for whom cross-bearing and forsaking everything have been required. We scarcely notice the words in the Te Deum – 'The noble army of martyrs praise thee' – praise as, for instance, in the words of this morning's psalm (Psalm 135). But suppose we think for just a few moments about the martyrs, the witnesses to Christ, beginning with those alive during the centuries when the texts that now form our New Testament were being read and preached and written. Those hearers heard such texts as our Gospel reading (and many others from the New Testament could be cited) in contexts where they might be harassed, brought before civil and religious authorities and done to death in the most dreadful ways. Persecution was sporadic and likely to be unsystematic but, as we know, it could get a hold, and very nasty it could be.

Turn back to our psalm again, and look at verses 15 and following. The idols of the heathen are man-made, dumb, blind, deaf and dead, and so are those who manufacture them, or indeed trust in them. A singularly unflattering assessment. Suppose then that one such idol is the image of the current emperor, and all that you are required to do is drop a pinch of incense on an altar in front of that image. If you were Jewish you had a sort of legal immunity from being required to do any such thing, but not if you belonged to some illicit new group – so-called Christians – that no one quite understood, the followers of a man done to death by the same authority now requiring you to drop a pinch of incense on an altar flame. Why on earth not do it? Why not save one's skin? The fundamental problem was, and remains, political allegiance, in the sense that saying some sort of Christian creed, however rudimentary, the Kyrie Eleison or the Sanctus or the Lord's Prayer ('thy kingdom come'), counts as refusal of the status quo. Christian allegiance lies elsewhere, not with the self-proclaimed lords of this world. Thus we find intolerable accounts of uncompromising Christians being pushed to the limits of life and out of it, rather than jeopardize the distinctiveness of their faith.

Read, if you have the stomach for it, the account of the martyrs of Lyons and Vienne in 177, and of the death of Blandina, of whom it was written that her fellow sufferers beheld in the form of their sister 'Him who was crucified for them, that He might persuade those who believe in Him that all who suffer for the glory of Christ have unbroken fellowship with the living God'. Or think of the commemoration of Perpetua and Felicitas (7 March), martyred in 203 in North Africa. Perpetua had to part with her infant son, whom she had taken to prison with her as she was breastfeeding him, handing him to her distraught father, and wrote up her experiences of imprisonment before entering the arena. Felicitas gave birth in prison, and her child was taken to be breastfed and reared by others. Their youth and their physical state when thrust into the arena horrified even the crowd who had assembled to watch them die. Perpetua's visions and prayer in prison had already brought her great consolation, since she had seen her unbaptized brother, dead as a result of cancer of the face at the age of seven, then happily playing with his face healed and his life transformed – a transformation brought about by her prayers and suffering. Utter refusal of parental authority, of home, children and the status quo, but believed by those who wrote up their story to be in Christ the means of salvation to others, the departed as well as the living.

And there, we may think, is the point of why they, and also others closer to our own time, need to be kept in mind. At the very least, they are examples of extraordinary courage – the kind we associate with soldiers – and we, of course, are not.

If we were, we might be having a very rough time of it somewhere or other. But you never know. When Oscar Romero (commemorated on 24 March) was a bright young seminarian, he could not have supposed that as Archbishop of El Salvador he would be murdered when celebrating the Eucharist in March 1980 because of his confrontation with some elements in his country's political regime.

That said, and courage apart, what all the martyrs have in common is something utterly Christ-like on which, finally, we need to focus when reflecting on this morning's Gospel. In the very next verse, 14.34 – also not set for reading but of great importance at this point – we find Christ saying, 'Salt is good'. If we want to know what salt symbolizes here, we need to think ahead in Luke's story. In the depths of what looks like utter disaster, Christ on the cross prays for the forgiveness of his tormentors. This is also central to those commemorated as martyrs: not just God-given courage, but the God-given capacity to change the worst experiences into a source of transformation for the whole human community, sometimes at huge personal cost. Our circumstances are mercifully different from those whose appalling vocation it was to be confronted by the words of Christ in the gospel and literally die by them. But surely trying to find the pinches of salt in the transforming power of forgiveness in our shared lives together is certainly required, and that at the very least we can draw from the call to discipleship of this morning's Gospel.

9

Avarice

Avaritia[1] – avarice! How rarely we use the word, so rarely that we might think we have no idea what it means. So let me begin by offering you a couple of examples to remind you, one biblical and one non-biblical.

When King David of Old Testament fame was caught out snatching Bathsheba and getting her husband bumped off in the front line of battle, he found himself visited by the prophet Nathan. Nathan got him without David being smart enough to spot the trap being set for him, by telling a story of a rich man and a poor man. The rich man was wealthy – that is to say, he owned flocks and herds and land on which to graze them. The poor man had just one little ewe lamb he'd bought and nourished. Later on it would be able to have its own lambs, and provide milk and wool, but in the meantime it lived with him and his family, eating and drinking with them and cuddled like a little daughter. The rich man had a visitor, and instead of killing one of his own animals to eat he took this little ewe lamb. And so he's condemned by David himself because he had no pity, at which point he convicts himself out of his own mouth. So there we are – power, desire, lack of restraint, ruthlessness. Instead of a relationship in which the rich man could at least have treated the poor man with some courtesy, and sometimes been generous – inviting him in to eat when he had a visitor, being beneficent and cheerfully kind, we have the possibility of such a relationship ruined by a heartless lack of

---

1 A reading was 1 Samuel 12.1–24, which does not appear in the Sunday readings in the RCL.

imagination. Quite apart from the fact that the story does not say that the poor man was even paid for his lamb, he's going to grieve for it as if it were a child he's nurtured. So, we begin to get the picture: avarice has to do with a whole personality, and it isn't an admirable one – who wants to be like that?

So to my second and non-biblical example. Remember Dodie Smith's wonderful story *One Hundred and One Dalmatians*?[2] Avarice there is personified in Cruella de Vil. She's rich, she's powerful, and she's used to getting what she wants. She embodies the 'must have' world we all live in. She already has a full-length, perfectly simple, pure white mink coat. But she has a brilliant idea for a new outfit – a black suit, and worn over it a stunning new coat made out of those enchanting black-spots-on-white dalmatian skins. So she buys dogs up, and if she can't buy them she kidnaps them. In the main incident in the story, she kidnaps a whole litter of 15 puppies. They're taken away to a kind of dog pound to grow up; and the bigger they get, the nearer they are to being killed. The parent dogs retrieve the lot, however, with the help of whole relays of equally courageous dogs. Cruella de Vil is arrogantly indifferent to the lives of other living creatures, wholly preoccupied with her own physical self-image, and of course she couldn't care less about the parent dogs grieving for their lost puppies, or the anxieties and grief of their owners. And how soon would she have got bored with a dalmatian-skin coat? What would she have wanted next?

We all recognize these pictures of human beings, and see what's wrong with them. They are driven by insatiable desires, no matter what the cost to others, and it's quite deadly to being even a half-decent person, let alone a wholly decent one. Nothing matters except the gratification of an awful sort of self – a particularly nasty form of idolatry (Colossians 3.5) – the worship of 'must have' for an awful sort of 'me'. Notice that the 'must have' isn't always money, though we'll come back to that. (Anyone ever thought of what we now refer to as 'status

2 Dodie Smith, *One Hundred and One Dalmatians* (Portsmouth, NH: Heinemann, 1956).

anxiety' as a form of avarice? Or how good our institutions are at producing it, and how difficult it is not to be ruined by desire to be given this or that form of recognition? Though I'm not going to pursue that issue here!)

I want to emphasize that between Nathan's parable and Dodie Smith's story there has been a lot of reflection down the ages on what the problem is. It first surfaces as a problem at the end of the first century of the Christian era, so far as Christian thinking is concerned, when it became clear that the 'end' of everything wasn't just around the corner, and that Christians had to live with goods and chattels. They had a lot of resources from their Jewish roots to help them – the practice of wiping off debts every so often so that people weren't destroyed by hopelessness; ways of caring for those who couldn't survive except by begging or stealing or selling themselves into prostitution or slavery; or those who were very vulnerable, such as widows, orphans, people with certain diseases, resident aliens, day labourers, people with disabilities – all those likely to be despised by the privileged. No wonder that when Christian Scripture came into being there was so much emphasis on almsgiving and hospitality, and those crazy parables of Christ's in which absolutely anybody can be dragged off the streets into a party. Of course, if we take grace, gift and God's unimaginable generosity to us seriously, what else would we expect?

Just how and why we don't behave the way we might expect became a matter of much sensitive self-questioning and self-criticism – which is why, by the end of the first millennium, the seven deadly sins had been pretty well identified – and always it's what serves good and harm in human relationships that's in focus. And avarice takes a new form in the second millennium when people begin more and more to deal with one another in cash transactions grown by trade. To begin with, cash related to land, flocks, herds, goods, precious stones, metals and all sorts of commodities. But increasingly it was negotiated by merchants and travellers: wealth associated with new groups of mobile people. Of course, people recognized that there was a lot of human ingenuity being put to good use – borrowing someone else's spare cash against one's own projected future wealth? But there were real worries too – what about money lent with interest to be paid back on it – usury? So some people had real power over others, and what was so worrying about that was that the job of handling it tended to be dumped onto merchants who were Jewish – so they became the focus of a lot of mistrust. This led not to a new form of avarice, but a near-relative, miserliness. So take this anecdote from medieval Islam (just to show you that the worries were justifiably widespread!). It depicts guests invited into their neighbour's home and taken aback at the strange behaviour of another of the guests. When dates and butter are served to the table around which the neighbours gather, one takes more than his share of the butter and rather than eating it lets it drip onto the table. The others remark that his share is greedy, his behaviour strange and wasteful. Another enlightens them: 'The table is his, and he wants to grease it in order to varnish it. He has divorced his wife, his children's mother, because he saw her washing a table of his with hot water. He said to her: "Why didn't you just wipe it?"'[3]

So we get avarice and miserliness linked together, and here's my last illustration:

And greedy Avarice by him did ride,
Upon a Camell loaded all with gold;
Two iron coffers hong on either side,
With precious metall full, as they might hold,
And in his lap an heape of coine he told;
For of his wicked selfe his God he made,
And unto hell him selfe for money sold;
Accursed usurie was all his trade,
And right and wrong ylike in equal ballaunce waide.

His life was nigh unto deaths door plast,
And thred-bare cote, and cobled shoes he ware,

3 Fedwa Malti-Douglas, *Structures of Avarice: The Bukhala' in Medieval Arabic Literature* (Leiden: Brill, 1985), 70.

Ne scarse good morsell all his life did tast,
But both from back and belly still did spare,
To fill his bags, and richess to compare;
Yet chylde ne kinsman living had he none
To leave them to; but through daily care
To get, and nightly feare to lose his owne,
He led a wretched life unto him self unknowne.[4]

Well, if he weren't such a menace we'd say he's a poor old thing, maybe. Idolatry, usury – we've all given up on that one – no difference between right and wrong, market values only, we might say; and he isn't even having fun. He looks as if he's at death's door, with an old coat, shoes long past the wearing, bad food, and no one he can think of to give it all to, rotten with anxiety, and he doesn't even know how miserable he is.

Doesn't look like us, exactly, does he? Well, at least I didn't arrive here on a camel, but I did come on an aeroplane; and I have enough spare cash in euros to keep a good number of starving children in Middle and Eastern Europe going for a bit, let alone homeless and parentless children in Afghanistan. And I'm deeply grateful for the management of my pension funds by the Universities Superannuation Scheme, which of course depends on the management of money making money – money now freelance, without ties to places or people or metals or commodities. Money's a commodity itself nowadays, tied up with transnational corporations and multinational companies, all of them representing claims against available resources, no matter what other claims there may be around. And I, like you, can't do without at least some of it; but we can keep thinking about what meaning it has for us, and whether we will let it ruin friendships, distort lives, shape our very desires, and influence our sense of what we think is good and right and true.

So how appropriate it is that we've thought about this in the clean-up time of Lent, the chance to reflect on our tastes, our desires, our cravings, and what we do about them. At the centre of our reflections must be a concern as to whether we

---

4 Edmund Spenser, 'The Faerie Queene' (1590).

have that mark of maturity, the capacity to say 'no' instead of 'must have'. And what will it take for us to be tactfully and gracefully generous, sensitive to how we appear to those less showered with wholly undeserved blessings as we are, self-critical and cautious about how we use power, willing to give charity where we know it can make such a difference. Anything, please God, to avoid being remotely like miserable, grisly old Avarice riding along on his camel.

IO

Spring (Easter)

Helen Waddell translated medieval Latin lyrics to make them available for readers in the twentieth century, and one of the most remarkable of these is a poem by Marbod of Rennes, with which I want to begin my reflections today. Marbod's lyric asks, 'Who can behold the earth's beauty without praising it?' When flowers bloom in thousands, woodlands flourish, birds of all kinds – blackbirds, jackdaws, magpies, nightingales – 'shout each other down' in praise. Marbod pictures people dancing, playing in lovely gardens, feasting through 'shining' summer days. 'So many lovely things', he says, must surely move us, put a smile on faces, soften moods, put us in touch with our hearts. And when we praise this loveliness, then we recognize the Maker, 'whose honour all these serve'.[1]

That's not quite Edinburgh, or Durham either, even a bit later in the year, but I hope you can catch in the poetry of an eleventh-century man some of the sheer *joie de vivre* that lies at the root of both of the readings we've heard this morning – the parable from Matthew and part of a letter from St Paul (1 Corinthians 15.19–26) – seedtime to harvest in their cases, so a bit further on into the summer than our poet. He starts, as our readings do, from the sense of joy we all have at the hums and buzzes and songs and smells and colours of a warm spring day, and the sheer thankfulness that it's all come round again, all happened again. We help some of it along, of course

---

1 This sermon was preached in an Eastertide context. A reading was Matthew 13.24–30, 36–43, appointed in the RCL for the Sunday between 17 and 23 July inclusive in Year C. The full poem is in Helen Waddell, *More Latin Lyrics: From Virgil to Milton* (London: Gollancz, 1976), 241.

– planting bulbs in autumn, changing our clothes, doing a little spring cleaning perhaps to match the shining newness of it all. But basically we rely on it just happening, a gift to us, as it inexhaustibly is – unless we make our surroundings just so awful and unpleasant that it simply can't get through.

The Gospel writer is alert to problems too. What about those tares in with the wheat that we have to put up with in the meantime, our confusions and difficulties – the tares muddle with the wheat in our hearts we might say. Sort it all out at the right time, the Gospel seems to say, so long as the growth goes on. What matters is the harvest. But Paul in his letter is using the metaphor of seed-time to harvest to make a somewhat different point. Here we are, receiving a page of a letter from him, and although we're in Edinburgh and not in Corinth, as it happens, we surely share the problem he's trying to grapple with. It's all very well, we might say after Easter – all that preaching about resurrection – but *how* are the dead raised up? And with what body do they come? So Paul has a shot at replying with talk of seed-time and harvest. And if we turn to chapter 12 of St John's Gospel, there's the metaphor again, and Jesus using it of himself: 'Truly, truly, I say to you, unless a grain of wheat falls into the earth and dies, it remains alone; but if it dies, it bears much fruit.' I say 'metaphor' meaning simply talking of one thing – that is, death and the promise of resurrection – in terms of another. What Paul tries to do is illuminate something we can't quite understand by means of something that we can, more or less.

I think that when those Corinthians asked, and ask for us, 'How are the dead raised up? And with what body do they come?' they're being very helpful – they're not asking an idle question just for the sake of it. They're voicing a real difficulty. And I'm not at all sure that talk of seed-time and harvest entirely meets it – how could it? The Corinthians know, as do we, that there's all the difference in the world between seeds and people. We don't pay a lot of attention to particular seeds one by one, or love them for themselves or mind when they're sown. But we do pay a lot of attention to one another, and damage one another very badly if we don't love one another into life. And that same attention and loving makes losing one another as we're 'sown' in death a matter of deep grief to us.

This is, I think, clearly expressed for us in our society by the film *Shadowlands*, about C. S. Lewis' life with his wife Joy, and his grief at her death. Behind *Shadowlands* lies the marvellous text he wrote called *A Grief Observed*, which takes us inch by inch through the pain of his loss, his having to let go of her. He learns to endure it until he gets to the point when he can love and praise God again, love and praise her again. He finds Joy and Joy's God present to him in some way, but with more to come, more to hope for. He wrote for Joy a poem that is very sombre as compared with my springtime poet, true for us when we've suffered grief and loss, but trying to express hope as well. At the particular place where her ashes are interred, the 'whole world' – stars, water, air, forest, field, the elements of earth that shaped Joy's life – are now 'like cast off clothes'. And yet this very place of ashes is also for him a place of hope – hope that 'holy poverty' learned in 'Lenten lands' might mean that cast off clothes would adorn Joy once more, on her 'Easter day'.[2]

Sombre, yes, but Lewis knows that we need our springtime poet too, for he starts with stars, water, air, field and forest – and so, we can say, does St Paul. He talks about seed-time and harvest, but also beasts, fishes, birds, sun, moon and stars, all with their own glory. What Paul is trying to do perhaps is keep alive in us the *joie de vivre* of springtime and seed-time in the form of hope that there's a harvest beyond the loss even of those most dear to us. It's a hope, a glimpse, a guess carried by the metaphor of seed-time that expresses the conviction not that God's love is as strong as death (as the Song of Songs speaks of human love) but that it's *stronger*. Harvest for us isn't something we might achieve for ourselves, but is what God promises to bring about as he is believed to have brought

---

2 Images of the memorial plaque with the full poem are easily found on the internet by searching keywords like 'Joy Davidman memorial Oxford Crematorium'. Read about the plaque in William Griffin, *Clive Staples Lewis: A Dramatic Life* (New York, NY: Harper and Row, 1986), 104.

it about for Jesus and as Lewis believed he would bring it about for his beloved Joy. Never easy to believe, and never easy to hope for – but that's perhaps precisely why we need to enjoy the springtime as our poet did, because springtime reawakens hope in us. As Psalm 126.5–6 has it: 'May those who sow in tears reap with shouts of joy! He that goes forth weeping, bearing the seed for sowing, shall come home with shouts of joy, bringing his sheaves with him.' Let us hope on this spring morning that indeed it may be so.

Pentecost

This morning we are going to consider together our reading from the Acts of the Apostles,[1] and I begin with a few basic observations about the book itself. As with most other books of the Christian Scriptures we have no precise knowledge of who wrote it, where it was written, or when it was written. But for various reasons we can surmise that it was written by whoever wrote the third Gospel – so we call the author of Acts by the same name – Luke, himself probably a Gentile. He writes for people who very largely share a common language, a kind of Greek that became common from the days of the conquests of Alexander the Great, sweeping across so many territories from his homeland in Macedonia to northern India, leaving behind in various places veterans from his army as settlers. This had the result that as far as the many scattered communities of Jews were concerned, it was essential to have Scriptures translated from Hebrew into Greek. Think again of that extraordinary list in the passage from Acts, detailing some of the places stretching East to West from which Jews had returned to live in Jerusalem, or come to visit for festivals. So that leaves us with a bit of a puzzle about what Luke thought had happened at Pentecost. Most people around at the time would in fact have been able to communicate in one way or another, given some patience and attention, no doubt in heavily accented Greek, depending on their origins. We'll come back shortly to what Luke proposes they actually heard on this occasion. Luke, however, is also writing at a time of some

---

1 Acts 2.1–21 is appointed for the Day of Pentecost in Years A, B and C of the RCL.

stability brought about by Roman conquest and occupation. It seems that he thought it worthwhile to try to commend to the authorities what was becoming a new religious movement of 'Christians', as they came to be called. So he wrote a kind of history of the beginnings of the movement for the benefit of those who might be persuaded that these Christians had some good news for them, and that Christians were likely to be good citizens.

The title is somewhat misleading. Luke has told us how the number of the twelve had been made up after Judas' death, but we hear nothing about most of the apostles, and reference to them as a group disappears from the narrative just over halfway through. The title of the book – Acts of the Apostles – does, however, remind us of their primary responsibility, which was to witness to Christ's resurrection and ascension, that most extraordinary turnaround from death and disaster to transformed life and the gift of salvation that inspires the first fragile Christian community. Our first reading from Ezekiel (chapter 17) is just one scriptural expression of the hope that God's Spirit could wholly transform a community, even one oppressed to the point of destruction.

In our reading the apostle Peter stands with the rest of the group of apostles and appeals to another Scripture – from the book of Joel – no less terrifying with its appeal to the sun being turned to darkness and the moon to blood. But at its heart is Peter's appeal to his hearers to recognize in the bubbling and ecstatic experience of noise and wind and licks of flame the presence of the divine Spirit in prophetic gifts for sons and daughters – the future – and the gifts of vision and dreams for the older members of the community without which little may be accomplished if things are to change.

The second half of Luke's history focuses on the apostle Paul, and we tend to give Paul a great deal of attention because of the letters and texts attributed to him that form a significant part of Christian Scripture. But in the first half of his history Luke reminds us that it is the apostle Peter who should be credited with making important moves in establishing both that the Christian movement springs from Jewish tradition – much gratitude for that, surely – and that it was good news for Gentiles as well (see the narrative about the conversion of Cornelius and his household in a later chapter). Luke also makes it clear that it was appropriate for Peter to set out the framework of Christian faith in speeches (as in the rest of chapter 2), crucially claiming that Christ having himself received the transforming divine Spirit is now the one who has bestowed it on those gathered at Pentecost. Such a speech comes to help shape the later credal claims of the Christian community – there are many examples of creeds in the first few centuries of the Christian era.

But why all this at Pentecost, we may well ask? Why the *fiftieth* day from Passover, and the end of the barley harvest, with the baking and enjoyment of barley loaves? It's because Pentecost is a time of celebration and gratitude to God for the harvest – holiday time. To quote one psalmist: 'Let the peoples praise thee, O God; let all the peoples praise thee! The earth has yielded its increase; God, our God, has blessed us' (Psalm 67.5–6). That's why the members of this new community described later on in the chapter as breaking bread from house to house, with gladness and singleness of heart, praising God. But there's even more to recall than the celebration of harvest, for Pentecost was also a time of celebration of God's gift of the Torah (a fundamental shape of salvation) on Sinai, a gift believed to have been given in every known language – a gift meant for everyone. So at this first Pentecost after the glorification of Christ, a renewed gift of salvation is again being offered to one and all, and that's what those gathered together hear. The differences between them are no longer allowed to separate them from one another, and they may be transformed simply by accepting the extraordinary gift they are offered. In the words attributed to Peter: 'it shall be that whoever calls on the name of the Lord shall be saved'.

And, finally, let us not underestimate the importance of visions and dreams – recall Elaine Paige and that song about a dream that life could be worth living, and the international impact of that song as Susan Boyle sang it. Or if you want an apostle comparable to Peter to voice it, recall 1963 and Martin

Luther King – a few words from a magnificent speech: 'I have a dream today, that the glory of the Lord shall be revealed, and all flesh shall see it together. This is our hope ... with this faith we will be able to hew out of the mountain of despair a stone of hope.'[2] I suggest that we might well say that 'the mountain of despair' is no resting place for Christian believers if we are to take to heart this morning's reading.

2 Martin Luther King, Jr, 'I have a dream ...', https://kinginstitute. stanford.edu/king-papers/documents/i-have-dream-address-delivered-march-washington-jobs-and-freedom (accessed 20.08.20).

12

Trinity

Depending on where and when you lived, in an earlier period of the history of the Christian Church, in the West at any rate, if you had turned up for a service on the Sunday after Pentecost you would have encountered some surprising differences from what you find today.[1] So one basic point I want to make right from the start is that if you are engaged with Christian liturgy – the prime source for most of us in learning Christian doctrine – you are inevitably and inescapably engaged with change, as insights develop and the tradition is engaged with different circumstances. This is as true of the Christian Church and its doctrines and traditions as it is of other long-lived elements of human culture, not least religious culture. And given that God is ultimately mysterious and inexhaustible and sometimes very much a 'God of surprises' (to use the title of a book published some time ago[2]), what else might we expect? Whatever we mean by 'revelation' it does not exclude necessary habits of reflection and prayer and the willingness to think things anew.

But the main issue here this morning is to do with Trinity Sunday, or some features of it as we have so far received it. Giving it attention at least once a year may help us to focus on its importance, rather than regard it as we sometimes do as another baffling item of tradition that we might just as well do without. Take the very title of today: Trinity Sunday. It takes its origin, apparently, from the fact that Thomas Becket (1119–70) wanted the day of his consecration, Pentecost Sun-

---

1 A reading was Isaiah 6.1–8, appointed in the RCL for Trinity Sunday, Year B.

2 Gerard W. Hughes, *God of Surprises* (London: Darton, Longman and Todd, 1985).

day, to be remembered – 'making a statement', as we might say, about the distinction between the authority of the Church and that of the monarch. Given that his consecration was later followed by his murder in that same cathedral (Canterbury), by the fourteenth century the commemoration of the day of his consecration was widely established (and not just in England). Given also the development of the last part of one major creed in general use that focused on the Spirit in the Church, the time was ripe for Pope John XXII in 1334 to establish Trinity Sunday on the existing day of commemoration, drawing to a conclusion the story of the incarnation while celebrating the Church's origins and authority – as indeed Becket himself might have wished!

So whereas it used to be the case that Pentecost was the key feast commemorating the sequence of events associated with the incarnation as the Church in both East and West sorted out its list of Scriptures and read that sequence, now there was an additional and explicitly doctrinal emphasis. There are, of course, differences in the Scriptures relating Ascension to Spirit-giving, but Pentecost 50 days after Easter celebrated the gift, and the innovation of Trinity Sunday related the gift of the Spirit to the Church as it had developed.

In addition, notice that if you had turned up to a Eucharist in the first thousand or so years of the Christian Church, you might not have encountered a creed as part of the liturgy. Creeds – and there were many of them in use – were primarily associated with baptism. At a baptism Christians committed or recommitted themselves to the vision of reality sketched out in a creed and put their hearts into what that might involve for them in their particular circumstances. Given that creeds sometimes featured in a Eucharist, however, it was not unreasonable for Pope Benedict VIII in 1014 to authorize the place of the creed we know in the Eucharist – and as I'll explain later, that was because he was being leant on by the then Holy Roman Emperor. As the reference to Becket indicated, what goes on in Christian liturgy sometimes had a lot to do with political pressures of one kind or another, odd though that may seem from our perspective.

One of the most significant occasions of political pressure, well before Becket's time, and setting an uncomfortable precedent, had resulted in the inclusion in a draft statement of belief – a creed in the making, one might say – of the phrase we find in our liturgy that Christ is 'of one substance with the Father'. It is a phrase to which we perhaps do not give enough attention. It was, so to speak, beaten into a draft statement of belief at a famous council summoned by the Emperor Constantine in 325. By that time Constantine had polished off his rivals and competitors, and was on the verge of transforming Byzantium into Constantinople. Having committed himself to supporting the new religious movement of the Christian Church, he wanted the bishops of his empire to finish with the controversy about Christ's relationship to God the Father – a very important issue for understanding and appropriating what was meant by 'salvation' and the security of salvation. So on 20 May 325, after some victory celebrations, the as yet unbaptized emperor presided over a conference at Nicea (modern Iznik), supported by his civil servants. As the bishops knew perfectly well, he was going to get their signatures on the document to be drafted, or their getting back home would be a somewhat distant prospect. The records of the meeting are problematic, to put it mildly, and no one knows who produced the key term, *homoousios* – 'being of one substance' – in Greek a word capable of multiple interpretations even by the Greek speakers present, never mind the Latin speakers, given different ways of relating Father/Son/Spirit together. To find a term of such ambiguity was a master-stroke – maybe provided by one of those civil servants? – so almost all the bishops signed, enjoyed an imperial banquet and imperial presents, went off to their different parts of the empire and went on arguing about the meaning of the term for many years. At that stage the statement of belief (probably based on the creed of the Jerusalem church) finished simply with the affirmation of belief in the Holy Spirit – full stop.

So there was likely to be more to come, and come it did in 381. Constantine was long since baptized and dead, and Emperor Theodosius was still struggling with some of his bishops at a meeting convened in Constantine's new capital Constantinople, minus bishops from the West and minus civil servants. The assembled company endorsed the moves made by the bishops at Nicea, which is why the creed incorporated into the Eucharist is rather sloppily referred to as the Nicene creed, which it is not – given the development of the third clause, on the Spirit, it is more properly referred to as the Nicene-Constantinopolitan creed.

There was to be one further development, nothing to do with imperial power in its origin, that you may notice if you look at that clause about the Holy Spirit – said in the creeds in use in the West to 'proceed' from the Father 'and the Son'. The nuisance phrase of the *filioque* is a source of continued disagreement between Western and Eastern Christians to this day (the Eastern Church prefers 'proceeds from the Father through the Son'). The 'filioque' came into existence perhaps as the result of an attempt to emphasize Christ's continued presence in the Church, though at the cost of introducing an element of 'subordination' in the Trinity where none was intended (the second clause had narrowly avoided the problem set up by the use of 'Father' and 'Son' by incorporating the phrase affirming that they are 'of one substance').

The phrase 'proceeding from the Father and the Son' seems to have originated in Toledo in the sixth century, and was incorporated into service books copied and distributed throughout what had become the Holy Roman Empire. Pope Leo III (796–816) could not be persuaded to add the phrase into the creed out of justifiable concern as to how this would further irritate relationships between West and East, so had the creed without the clause inscribed on two silver shields put up at the tomb of St Peter. The papacy lost out to the Holy Roman Emperor of the day (Henry II) when Benedict VIII (1012–24) was leant on to incorporate the phrase into the now well-developed creed when he needed imperial troops to fight some of the papacy's battles.

And there is one final innovation to note, for in the consecration prayer, beyond the so-called words of institution, there is a prayer to God the Father to send the Holy Spirit on the congregation and the bread and wine so that these become the body and blood of the Son. That invocation too would not have been present in earlier versions of the consecration prayer, in the West at least. If we stop to think about it, however, we can see that there is a certain incoherence between the third clause of the creed as we have it, with the Spirit proceeding 'from the Father and the Son' and the consecration prayer to the Father to send the Spirit, whereas if we did away with the 'filioque' the difficulty would not arise.

This particular development of the liturgy has come about not as the result of political pressure in the sense of pressure from state authorities but presumably as the result of deeper appreciation of the criticism of the Eastern Church, that despite the *'filioque'* phrase there was something of critical importance missing from Western theology and eucharistic liturgy in particular – the significance of the Spirit.

So, that is part of the story of how we come to have a Trinity Sunday, a Sunday dedicated to a doctrine summarizing both gospel events and their consequences, with the doctrine itself sometimes developing in what must seem to us to be surprising circumstances. The main point I want to make, though, is that if we are part of a living tradition, as insights change and we learn from one another and from maybe surprising sources and strange circumstances, we should expect – and even nerve ourselves not to fear or resent – change in liturgy. Indeed, we need to find the courage to hope for it and to welcome it. And strange though that may seem, to me it is the very doctrine of the Trinity itself – given its innovative and one might say experimental, controversial character as the creed sketches it – that might help to cheer us into thinking constructively about how we worship in future years.

13

Holy Man of Galilee

'Jesus went about all the cities and villages, teaching in their synagogues and preaching the gospel of the kingdom, and healing every disease and every infirmity' (Matthew 9.35).[1]

This morning we are focused on the reading from the first Gospel and the clues it gives us to the character of a certain holy man from Galilee, Jesus of Nazareth. Matthew gives us some of the memories of Jesus' disciples – retellings of parables, instructions, proverbs and activities – shifted from Aramaic into a sort of colloquial Greek, then from speech to writing, from source to document, and into a new style of memory-making Gospels eventually attached to the priceless inheritance of the Hebrew Scriptures. In the case of the Gospel from which we are reading, it's worth guessing where it was written. It used to be thought its origin was in Syria, but it is now thought to have been written in Galilee itself, and it certainly gives us some remarkable glimpses of Jesus of Galilee and the impression he made on his contemporaries.

Galilee in his time was rural, agricultural – shepherds and farmers provide lively illustrations in his teaching. It was known for tough fighters, likely to be rebellious, and a source of concern to those responsible for keeping the peace in what was occupied territory; the people were religiously somewhat uneducated, living in hamlets and villages about an hour's walk from one another, and with a few insignificant townships. As it so happens, Galilee was the location where the earliest

---

1 A reading was Matthew 9.35—10.23, appointed for the Sunday between 12 and 18 June inclusive in the RCL, Year A.

group of rabbis were to be found. It was also associated with some prophets of earlier times, notably Elijah – a true prophet known as one who loved the Lord his God with all his heart and soul, to quote Deuteronomy 13.3. And we remember that Elijah appears with Moses at Jesus' 'transfiguration'. As for Moses, Jesus too was clearly a memorable teacher – some of it sorted and themed in the first part of our Gospel, some of it found in the teaching of his disciples throughout the Gospel.

If we attend to the details, of course, Jesus is very much his own man. He sits light to custom and traditions of how to 'walk-travel' through life as a Jew of his day; he shares meals with all sorts and conditions of humanity, and he becomes something of an irritant to those in authority. Nonetheless, he's recognized as a 'son of David' – which means not his family ancestry but recognition as a second Solomon; Solomon (in 1 Kings 4.29) was endowed not simply with wisdom and understanding but with 'largeness of heart' or, as one translation has it (JB), 'a heart as vast as the sand on the seashore', and in tradition, a great healer.

So Jesus was remembered not just as a teacher who gathered a group of disciples around him – essential to his mission – but as a healer, and Matthew states the connection twice, once at 4.23 and then in our reading (9.35). He's a man of great gifts, sometimes burdensome – it's no accident that he sometimes heads off into the hills by himself. There were other men with some of those gifts – we know the name of a near contemporary, Hanina ben Dosa, another exorcist. And in Jesus' time, healing bodies, restoring minds, forgiving sins, expelling demons, preaching repentance (the turn-around needed) were, so to speak, interchangeable, and all connected in the Lord's Prayer – the insistence that God's name is to be sanctified, God's reign established, our essential needs supplied, the availability of forgiveness, and a prayer for protection.

Our reading concludes three sections in this Gospel on Jesus' miracles and instruction to Jesus' disciples. And we're given an important clue in the second verse of our reading (9.36) where we hear that Jesus is 'moved with compassion'. Remember Solomon, with a heart as vast as the sand on the seashore?

Translations that tell us that Jesus 'felt sorry' for or 'had pity' on someone or other – crowds of people in this case – don't do justice to what is said of Jesus here: the gut-wrenching capacity to imagine, feel deeply, to embody 'loving-kindness' to others, the determination to ease their lot in life, seeing them like sheep without a shepherd, an ungathered harvest, badly led, uncared for. And his well-instructed disciples are now to act as he does, some of them apparently with his gifts to exorcize evil, to heal. They are to carry some of his burdens, moving from place to place, sometimes rejected, sometimes accepted, starting with those already identified as 'lost sheep' – the strays of the parable that turns up later in this Gospel.

The writer knows what may happen both to them and to their successors, sent out as sheep in the midst of wolves – conflict, opposition – and the second part of our reading switches from a focus on Jesus' disciples to describe what the consequences of their mission would turn out to be: to a focus on the communities where there would be bitter dispute within Jesus' own tradition about whether indeed it was the case that God's reign was close at hand in the person of Jesus, his teaching and actions, and those of his disciples. Those disputes had terrible consequences in later years.

I suggest that what we might take from our Gospel is a focus on Jesus' compassion, a heart as vast as the sand on the seashore, and attend to what is actually going on around us, seeking our own response to it, which may well invite conflict and opposition at least some of the time. There is a lot in our society to encourage us to back off, not even to ask questions, to identify responsibility. Yet mission for us, in our time, just might require us, for example, to ask questions about why some of our fellow citizens are housed in tower blocks too tall for firefighters to reach when things go hideously wrong, quite apart from the provision of water-sprinklers, fire-proofed staircases and doors, well-rehearsed exit drills – I don't need to labour the point. What are we saying about ourselves if we don't even ask? And if that is the case, how do we think we are keeping faith with a man with a heart as vast as the sand on the seashore?

14

Taking a Stand

This evening's reading from the book of Amos (9.5–15) reminds us of the creative power of God, of his care for all the peoples of the earth.[1] It insists on God's determination to establish justice – there's that disturbing image of being shaken in a sieve to keep in mind. And it ends with promises – harvest, vineyards, inhabited cities, fruitful gardens, a planted people. The book of Amos was of course 'Scripture' for early Christian communities, and remained so when there emerged agreement about what else was going to count as authorized reading. And at the end of the first century of the Christian era the new communities who heard and read Amos found themselves in very different circumstances from his. What then were they to make of divinely given promises?

The author of our second text this evening was clearly indebted to Paul the apostle, and honoured his memory by writing his address in Paul's name. He continues some of Paul's lines of thought, but is courageous enough to think things through in a situation different not only from the age of Amos, centuries before, but different from the situation in which Paul the apostle worked. And in our author's time, it did indeed look as if the sieve of judgement had been given a good shaking, because Christian communities were having to make sense of the fall of Jerusalem and the destruction of its temple, and the destruction of towns and villages and countryside by Roman imperial power in the year 70 as we now date it. What do God's promises look like in this new context?

---

1 A reading was Ephesians 1.3–14, appointed in the RCL for the Second Sunday after Christmas, Years A, B and C, and the Sunday between 10 and 16 July inclusive, Year B.

And what could it all have to do with the divine promise given particular embodiment in the incarnation, crucifixion, resurrection, ascension and Spirit-giving of the one now addressed as 'the Lord' Jesus Christ? What was a community gathered for worship of Christ to make of the events they had witnessed?

The central point our author commends to his hearers was that because the temple was no more, the boundary walls in the temple precincts which divided people from one another were also no more. This meant, or should have meant, that non-Jews (Gentiles) were no longer aliens and strangers, but themselves now members of God's household, a new kind of temple, and a new focus for the worship of God. This new temple, this 'church', was built on the foundation of apostles and prophets, was held together by Christ, and was given life by the creative and re-creative Spirit of God. We heard in Amos of God's care for all peoples, and we can think also of the promises to Abraham, that he was to be the source of blessing for all the families of the earth.

Here in the new Christian community the meaning of that promise of blessing was being made evident even in and through the tragedy of rebellion and defeat. So our author began his address with a blessing: 'grace and peace from God the Father and our Lord Jesus Christ'. And here, alone in the new Scriptures, Christ is referred to as 'the Beloved', perhaps recalling the divine words at Christ's baptism and transfiguration: 'Thou art my beloved Son; with thee I am well pleased' (Mark 1.11). The address as a whole is, I suggest, trying to work through the implications of that trust in 'the Beloved'.

Our author then moves from blessing to thanksgiving, for he has much to say about the grace lavished on the Christian community, not least the provision of time and space to reconsider their troublesome relationships: not just with Jewish Christians, but the much more difficult problem of relationships with the Jews who did not become Christians, and who remained inheritors of divine promises. And then: their troublesome relationship with one another. For if they are a new kind of temple, a 'church' indeed, made one with 'the Beloved' in baptism – given a stamp or seal of a new identity by God's

Spirit, made *corpus Christi*, Christ's body – they really have to sort themselves out. They have to shed the habits of edgy, quarrelsome, grudging outsiders, and they have to acquire the habits of the included, the generosity of those loved. What is it for them, for us, to become and live as the 'body' of 'the Beloved' one?

As we know, the Church is not for those who want only the company of those we think are like-minded, not for those who spend their time admiring themselves in the lives of others. As our author points out, there are varieties of gifts in the Church, and he happens to list those needed to secure the foundations: apostles, prophets, evangelists, pastors and teachers – a list one might paraphrase as including entrepreneurs, questioners, story-tellers, systematizers, or movers and shakers, finishers and fixers, and they certainly won't get on with one another unless they work at it! We could make our own list of what a community or institution needs if it is going to adapt and flourish through time, and in our author's view the Church is in it for a long haul. Whatever their gifts, they are going to have to interplay with one another, the way our joints and sinews at best do in our own bodies, but it needs effort and attention. Thus blessing, thanksgiving, understanding and working at relationships – in the body of 'the Beloved' – means that we don't just talk it, we have to walk it; as our author puts it, 'walk in love' as children of light, which is to say, we have to become those whose lives will stand scrutiny.

Our reading this evening comes in partway through our author's suggestions and advice, and we won't necessarily agree with everything he suggests. For instance, just what could we make of advice relevant to slave-owning households, and the profound distortions of relationships integral to the very fact of owning and being owned by another person? We have to acknowledge that it is in part because we find the sort of advice we have in our reading – how to negotiate relationships between slaves and slave owners – that it took Christians a very long time to understand the implications of baptism, of becoming the body of 'the Beloved'. And it took us too long by far to realize the iniquity of trading in the lives of others, and surely it is to our bitter shame that trading and trafficking of people in and from poor and disrupted societies is still so prevalent, so inevitable unless we stop it. Why do we close our eyes to trafficking in babies and young children, as well as adults desperate for work and a decent life? It is not enough for us now to say that our author did his best to give thoughtful advice in what looked like a society that could not change. Both he and we need a more fundamental, more radical, stance.

Perhaps to our astonishment, that is what our author offers us in conclusion. For after all that he has said about love and peace, forbearance and self-effacement in life with 'the Beloved', he urges his hearers and readers to put on the whole armour of God, and to 'stand'. He's drawing here on Scripture, for the splendid passage in Isaiah 59.14–19 is one source for what he says, and the invitation is to put on the armour God wears, as God seeks justice. This invitation is addressed to the whole Church – many gifts, one Church; many pieces of armour, one Church. Mercifully no one person has to bear the burden of 'stand', or taking a stand, but 'stand' on some issues we certainly do need to do. I've referred to trading and trafficking in human life as just one example. And, to conclude, in order to do that, we have to take seriously our author's one further injunction if we seriously want to align ourselves with God's search for justice. For we are urged to pray with perseverance, praying not just for courage but for the stamina and intelligence and resources we need to become the Church of 'the Beloved', which exists, after all, not for itself but for the sake of the world that God judges, loves and saves.

15

God's Reign in our Affairs

I want to comment on just one verse, Colossians 1.24, where the writer – probably Paul – informs his hearers and readers: 'I rejoice in my sufferings for your sake, and in my flesh I complete what is lacking in Christ's afflictions for the sake of his body, that is, the church.'[1]

Let's start at the end, with the analogy of the Church as Christ's body, one of many such analogies. It's meant to indicate that being part of Christ is something like being part of a living organism – all the arms and legs and head and torso and whatever we like to specify has its function so that everything fits together, and at best works harmoniously. There can even be the splendid cooperation and grace we may see nowadays perhaps in a crack athlete or dancer or skater, or team player, with everything in superb order, ready to explode with energy to entertain others or to compete with them, to smash a record or win a medal. But the analogy of the body is not being used here to give us the reassuring image of cooperation and co-inherence with others in superb form. The analogy here is connected with what for us is a far less attractive feature of being part of the body of Christ, and that is the ability not merely to meet or bear affliction but to rejoice in it, and to have the courage to believe that it can have its place, its point in life: 'in my flesh I complete what is lacking in Christ's afflictions for the sake of his body, that is, the church'.

Earlier in the letter Paul has written about Christ's all-sufficiency, and he is not abandoning what he said earlier on.

---

1 A reading was Colossians 1.15–28, appointed in the RCL for the Sunday between 17 and 23 July inclusive in Year C.

Neither he nor we have any part in the 'work' of Christ, though many people are able to find their life given meaning by his identification with them, in all their vulnerability and suffering. What Paul is trying to do is to sort out some muddle in the church to which he is writing, the kind of muddle we might well get into when we attempt to understand and appropriate for ourselves what 'completing' what is lacking in Christ's afflictions might mean. So what seems to have gone wrong in the community to which Paul writes, and can go wrong for us, perhaps thinking that we can train ourselves to complete what is lacking in Christ's afflictions?

The point may be that when we have reached the stage of knowing perfectly well that we really have to tackle our habits of self-indulgence, the pain of self-discipline can easily become an end in itself. We can become hooked on it, even use it as self-punishment, and forget the goal of it, which is to become more open to others and to God. It may become precisely an exercise in the self-indulgence we were trying to be rid of, in that we are simply even more self-preoccupied than we were before. We can even find ourselves soliciting applause for our efforts, whereas being reassured that we're the greatest thing since sliced bread simply isn't part of the deal. We have to get on with changing bad habits without feeling that everyone loves us and wants us and thinks we're wonderful. And if we can't, we're hardly ready even to begin – but to begin what? Being open to others and to God or, as Paul puts it, for the sake of the Church, or more precisely for the sake of what the Church is meant to stand for – the reign of God in our affairs.

We might at this point take Paul as an example of one of the blessed in St Matthew's version of the so-called 'sermon on the mount'. For Paul hungers and thirsts for the righteousness of God to prevail. We might not agree all the time with the way he thought this should work out in practice, even if we could fully comprehend what he was talking about; and in any case, nowadays he might work some things out rather differently – or we hope he would – but we should at least try to attend to what he was after. So far as we know, Paul did not go around looking for emotional and physical affliction for its own sake, but equally important he wasn't frightened of affliction either. He rejoices in what comes his way, not because he likes what happens to him but because it comes about in the course of his struggle for the reign of God, and the conflicts he's tripped into as a result, without seeking them. And he finds the courage to rejoice because he's confident that what he does – even if he sometimes gets it wrong – is done for God's sake, and because he knows that he's supported by the love and prayers of others who have the same end in view: the reign of God in our affairs.

Of course, it can often look as though absolutely nothing is being served by affliction, least of all the reign of a loving and righteous God. What could look worse than Christ's affliction on the cross, after he has prayed, 'O righteous Father'? And it is a hard and bitter lesson to learn that there are circumstances in the world about which nothing can be done. Christ's body was not released from the cross until he was dead. Completing what is lacking in Christ's afflictions may be nothing more or less than patient and unprotesting acceptance of injustice and apparent pointlessness if we are on the receiving end; and doing all we can in our turn to support and care for those who are on the receiving end when we, personally, are not. That, however, should never, ever, be used to persuade people to go in for victimization, the self-degradation of those who seem to opt for what they think is affliction but is more a kind of self-chosen pain and isn't likely to be of service to anyone else, let alone to God. Some possibilities are marked: 'Don't go there'.

Paul is not talking about self-degradation or self-victimization, or collusion in injustice that can be remedied. More likely he is talking about the kinds of risk of pain that comes to those who stand up to be counted in an unjust world because they are gripped by a vision of a better one. It is that vision that enables people to behave generously and lovingly – even joyfully – when they have suffered more than most of us, we hope, are ever likely to. Take, for example, the staggering prayer found by the body of a child in an extermination camp in the 1940s and not inappropriate in parts of the world today:

Lord, remember not only the men and women of good-will, but also those of ill-will. But do not remember all the suffering they have inflicted on us: remember the fruits we have bought, thanks to this suffering – our comradeship, our loyalty, the greatness of heart, which has grown out of all this, and when they come to judgement, let all the fruits which we have borne be their forgiveness.

Completing what is lacking in Christ's afflictions won't come to anything so terrible for us, we hope; but let us hope that we manage to respond with comparable generosity to whatever comes our way when we try – if we do, as we should – to establish in our own lives what Paul was trying to work out in his. And, above all, somehow to find the courage to be joyful about it, when it is a sign of the revolution in human affairs Christ died to bring about.

16

Suffer the Children

In case it hasn't occurred to you, let me begin by saying that Christianity in its origins in connection with Jesus of Nazareth is not a family-oriented religion, to put it mildly.[1] That very point helps to highlight the fact that children were all the same very important to Jesus. He may, for all we know, have been acutely sensitive to the fact that it was a sort of miracle that they were born alive in the first place, and that their mother survived their birth, if they did. We forget all too easily with our expensive, high-tech medical services just how dangerous the whole business of childbirth actually is. If he'd ever been married, as one might expect of a young Jew of his time, it's just possible that he'd lost a young wife and a baby himself. It might account in part for his footloose life.

Whatever we make of all that, he seems to have realized how precious children are in a human community, each of them one-off, irreplaceable – the religious word is 'sacred'. And when Jesus wants to make a point about his own identification with the 'least' in the world he takes a child and sets him by him. Receive the child, receive Jesus; receive Jesus, and receive God (Luke 9.48). Cut it even shorter and just say, receive a child and receive God. It's much the same point as in the 'suffer little children' passage we've just heard (Luke 18.16), except that this time it's not Jesus reaching for a child but rebuking those of his disciples who are trying to prevent people bringing children to him, so he can touch them – whatever that means. Perhaps an act of blessing, perhaps a hug from a man without

---

1 A reading was Luke 18.15–17, which does not appear among the Sunday readings in the RCL.

children of his own. Perhaps a blessing given by hugging. We could say that he knew how important it was for children to be hugged and cuddled and given lots of physical affection. Starve them of it and they grow up very cross and very destructive, deeply unsure of whether they can be lovable to themselves, to others, and to God. It's very important not to lose sight of that. Perhaps he let people see that he minded not having his own children around, and the word got around, especially to those mothers and fathers grieving over dead or dying children, or over living but damaged children. They might not have found the courage to bother him otherwise. There's no 'for adults only' sign up here, it really does look as if he really liked them. And before we think why that might be the case, let me emphasize that this has nothing to do with being unrealistic about them. Children can be insatiably demanding, smelly, spotty, runny-nosed, crying, cross and sleepless, wilful and argumentative and impossible to please – all that, and more. Spare a thought sometime for those who have got you this far. Crucially, in addition, they are likely to be spontaneous, eager, curious, fingers into everything, finding out how things work.

What Jesus particularly seems to have liked is their capacity to ask for and like presents – give me an egg, give me a fish, Dad – have a look at Matthew 7.9–10, and Dad can often think of something better, he says. It's an important point: if you know how to give good gifts to your children, that gives you a clue to how God deals with us, through lavish presents – some of the time anyway. In Christian language, it's called grace. And hence, incidentally, the baptism of infants: God's capacity to give, responding to a child's limitless capacity to receive. Unfortunately, children's very openness makes them acutely vulnerable, and their innocence is no protection if Dad can think of something worse – a stone instead of an egg, a scorpion instead of a fish. Where it's the worst rather than the best on offer, the damage can be considerable. And offering children the worst is a potential in all of us – you, me, everyone. We're not thinking here of someone other than ourselves. If we offer children the best, it's not because we're incapable of giving them the worst, but perhaps because there are restraints or constraints on us, not least that we've learned that self-gratification is not a principal good in life. Saying 'no' to what we might fancy, or think we fancy, is a mark of maturity, especially if we might harm a child by indulging ourselves.

You might think that's all very obvious. If so, how do we account for the fact that in 1883 it became clear to a group of concerned people that we needed a Society, now a National Society, for the Prevention of Cruelty to Children? We could pursue the same question by asking about the founding of Save the Children, but we'll stay with the era of the NSPCC. Recall also that just two years later, in 1885, a piece of legislation was passed that raised the age of consent to sexual intercourse for female children from 13 to 16 as part of a move to discourage the sale of girls into prostitution, and to protect the young from sexual predators generally. In its founding days, the NSPCC was particularly concerned with children at work, scraping a living on the streets – children more or less in the public eye. It took roughly another 70 years to face up to the domestic horrors of children starved, burned and battered in their own homes. You can track it in the medical literature, especially associated with the name of C. Henry Kempe of the USA.

How convenient, you might think, if we could dump it all on the medics. But we can't make them our consciences in this area – they do the mopping up, and may be able to go beyond that by triggering off further intervention. One of the reasons it's so difficult to face is that it is tricky to know what to do when a child has been physically damaged. In particular, remember that it was no longer possible for medics to ignore what was happening to some children with the advent of X-rays, tracing the breaks in the bones, the evidence of children having been shaken into death. Spare a prayer sometimes for those whose exasperation and exhaustion and inexperience with children precipitate the wreckage.

What I want briefly to talk about is another matter that has to do with whether children are safe in their own homes, and that is their sexual abuse. We have known for a long time in this country, and not just via 'sex tourism' as it is so nauseatingly called, that people in charge of children can abuse them sexually, either themselves, or earning money by letting others do so. This includes women as well as men, though it seems mostly to be men. And by men here I mean predominantly heterosexual men – it seems to be primarily their power in households and institutions of various kinds, including church-related ones, that's being expressed through the sexual abuse of children with no cash involved. So a century on, another society was formed, called Christian Survivors of Sexual Abuse, whose first national meeting was held in York in 1993. But don't for one minute think that the problem is a new one, or that it never happens in Christian households or institutions of one kind or another – it's not just folklore, but legends of the sufferings of some of the saints that give us clues to its prevalence in the past. And it may be at its worst when adults think they are answerable to no one for their behaviour to children, where they think they 'own' them, or where they think they have special authority over them, that the problem may arise. If that's how adults think and feel, they're certainly a long way from the sort of attitude to children I suggested at the beginning we might find exemplified in Jesus of Nazareth. It's a problem of the expression of power over others, with the other being very vulnerable, and self-gratification at the core of it.

How sexual abuse affects children varies, and the damage may be to their emotions and to their imaginations rather than to their bodies. Surfing the internet and finding pornography would be one example. But it's their bodies that are 'the scene of the damage' – it's the body that remembers, the body that works out strategies for survival, the body that learns to numb pain; so let's think about bodies, if we can. The five most harmful factors seem to be the following, beginning with the body: bodily penetration whether oral, anal or vaginal; the persistence of the abuse; the abuse of trust involving a main 'carer' in the child's life; the use of force or threat of it if a child can't be groomed or seduced into compliance; and a negative response to a child who breaks through the walls of secrecy that surround the abuse to tell someone what is happening.

The younger and more vulnerable the child, the more difficult it may be to persuade someone to listen, but older children and children grown up, like yourselves, may also be met with denial. Of course there may be false accusations, of course there may be false memories – people will sometimes find any apparent explanation for why they feel so awful – but we can, with practice, learn to sort all that out. What is the initial, right response? It's also five-fold: I believe you; I am glad you came to me; I am very sorry this happened; it is *not* your fault; together we are going to get some help and do something about it. We haven't time to pursue the options, but let me conclude with a few very important things to bear in mind.

The road out is not signposted at the very beginning of getting over it with the magic words 'forgive and forget'. Nothing could be more deadly. There is a place for these words at the end, but not, repeat not, at the beginning. The beginning is *remember*; not bodies, now, but brains: think, recall, get a life-raft afloat by trying to get straight what happened. This may be emotionally painful as feelings are allowed to surface, and people need to find words for their rage – there's some good stuff in the Psalms, especially the bits we like to cut out nowadays. Anger tells us how bad it was, but it needs to go along with belief in an all-seeing God from whom injustice is never hidden. That's why, when we reach the limits of human justice, the problem can be dumped on God. And at the end of the process, it may be possible to let go, move on. And if you're still not sure about how deadly the sexual abuse of children may be, remember how we started: receive a child, receive Jesus; receive Jesus and receive God. Substitute 'abuse' for receive and you'll see the point – abuse a child, abuse Jesus; abuse Jesus and abuse God. Very unpleasant, isn't it? But it's a way of reminding us what's at stake here, how much it matters. Cheer up, though, and remember the divine promises of abundance, grace, generosity and blessing – and let's see how we can make it possible for children to learn all that. A bit of Christ-like behaviour now and then would be the place to start.

17

Wiping Away Tears

Our first reading this morning, from the book of Isaiah (25.6–10),[1] provides us with an opportunity for two lines of reflection, both important. The first is concerned with the placing of the book of Isaiah itself in Christian liturgy and tradition. The second is concerned with the importance of this morning's reading for our beliefs – and the one follows on from the other.

Take the centrality of the book of Isaiah in Christian liturgy and tradition first – something, we remind ourselves, we share in common with the synagogue liturgies of Judaism, as one might expect given the roots of Christian worship in the living tradition of Judaism. Especially in the run-up to Advent it is worth attending to the book of Isaiah, for our Advent liturgies especially draw very heavily on it – consider all those texts and antiphons that are concerned with Christ's having come from the root of Jesse, Christ being the key of David, and the longing for the presence of God with us: Immanuel. It's all together wrapped up in the hymn, 'O Come, O Come Immanuel'. And even if we don't pay much attention to Christian liturgy, we may well enjoy a performance of Handel's *Messiah*, or 'sing-along' in one of its performances around this time – and that will teach us texts from Isaiah if nothing else does, not least some of the words from this morning's reading. I'll come back to that in a minute.

Let us focus to start with on why the book of Isaiah became and remained so important. The answer fundamentally is that

---

1 This reading is appointed in the RCL for Easter Evening in Years A and C, and in Year B also for Easter Day and All Saints – none of which are the context in which this sermon was preached ('the run-up to Advent').

from the earliest years of Christianity the prophet who gave the whole book of Isaiah its name – that person was deemed to have foreseen the arrival of the anointed one: the Messiah, the Christ, someone of special importance in God's presence with and among humankind. For there were words that Isaiah the prophet had addressed to the king, Ahaz, in the besieged city of Jerusalem, the mountain city of our reading this morning: words of promise that by the time a young woman – Ahaz's wife, probably – had conceived and borne a son, Immanuel, the sign of God's continuing presence, the city would be free of its enemies. These words, as we recall, were picked up by the writer of our first Gospel, Matthew, to interpret the meaning of the message given by an angel to Joseph in a dream, about the significance of the child to be born to Mary, Joseph becoming the interpreter of that text of Isaiah. Matthew was here simply doing what the Christians of his day, and before his day, were in the habit of doing, which was finding in their Scriptures – which were of course the Scriptures of their Jewish friends and neighbours and fellow worshippers – the language by which they could express and interpret what was going on. From as early as the second century, in one of the catacombs in Rome we find Isaiah in a wall painting near to a representation of Mary with her child on her lap, Isaiah pointing to them: Christ sprung from the root of Jesse. And he points also to a star near them, the star out of Jacob from another book, Numbers (24.17) – the star of Matthew's second chapter, which guides the mysterious magi on their way.

So he's Isaiah the prophet, but he became known as an evangelist too – the fifth evangelist, indeed – for two reasons. One is that there are some 250 quotations from or allusions to the text of Isaiah in Christian Scriptures – from Matthew to the book of Revelation. But the other is that it became a tradition to write up the whole narrative of Christ's life and its meaning – from incarnation to last judgement – in the language of Isaiah. And what is important about this is that understanding Christ in and through the language of Isaiah may well have its origin in Christ's own struggle for understanding his relationship to God, his mission and the meaning of his own death and resurrection. Read Isaiah, then, and we get clues to Christ – at least, that is how some of our earliest Christian writers understood the matter. The words of a great prophet, a great poet, a person of the most profound insight, take us at least part of the way to understand Christ, perhaps even close to the way Christ understood himself.

Although nowadays we are no longer familiar with that way of approaching the significance of Christ – and maybe we could learn a great deal from it – the habit of alluding to Isaiah continues to provide us with phrases of great importance to us, even now: beating swords into ploughshares, wolves and lambs getting on with one another, voices crying in the wilderness, good news for the poor, the promise of a new heaven and a new earth, the desire for a house of prayer for all nations, to mention but a few – not forgetting 'there is no peace for the wicked', which must mean us at least some of the time, for if we are never troubled by our conscience we really are in trouble! And of course, at the heart of the Christian Eucharist is the praise of the holiness of God drawn from the prophet's own vision – the conviction that the whole earth manifests the divine beauty and authority: 'Holy, holy, holy, Lord God of hosts, heaven and earth are full of thy glory', which was part of Christian worship from the fourth century of our era.

Given all this, why is our reading from chapter 25 so important? It's because Isaiah promises what Christ in resurrection, ascension, Spirit-giving and presence in word and sacrament actually embodies, which is the universal vision of the prophet, the salvation of all, not just as a promise (though promise in a sense it remains), but as something at least as good as the most splendid feast or celebration one could imagine in a restored city, free at last of threats – plenty of those threats around at the moment – and free even of death. On this mountain God will remove the mourning veil covering all peoples, and the shroud enwrapping all nations. He will destroy death for ever. 'The Lord will wipe away the tears from every cheek.' Paul, in the fifteenth chapter of the first letter to the Corinthians where he struggles to explore the meaning of resurrection, writes, 'O death, where is thy sting? O grave, where is thy victory?'

– words crucial to the third part of Handel's *Messiah*. And
the writer of that ferocious book Revelation twice uses this
passage of Isaiah, once in 7.17 and notably in chapter 21: 'God
shall wipe away all tears from their eyes; and there shall be no
more death, neither sorrow, nor crying, neither shall there be
any more pain (KJV).'

To ask an obvious question: does our human world look
like God's feast on the mountain? To say the least: not unam-
biguously. It does not, and there are enough charitable appeals
coming through our letter-boxes to remind us of the fact, even
if we personally don't have to face mega-threats of worldwide impact at present. Isaiah, however, could not have been
the prophet and 'evangelist' that he was unless he had been
prepared, as we must be, to be as honest, clear-sighted and
perceptive as we may be, graced by God, about ourselves and
our responsibilities. We're not nearly as helpless as we might
like to think as we try to wriggle out of doing what we must
and can. With some clarity we might just recapture some of
Isaiah's vision of a universal salvation. We cannot destroy
death – only God can – but we can make life a lot better for
many, and we can wipe away a lot of tears. We need to lift our
eyes beyond the very real threats that so concern us, and do
what we can to realize a little of that vision of his, at once his,
and in Christ very much ours.

18

The Face of Christ

From the reading of 2 Corinthians 4, keep a few words and phrases especially in mind:

Christ as the image of God
the face of Christ
light ... knowledge ... grace ... glory

and in particular, verse 6:

For it is the God who said, 'Let light shine out of darkness,' who has shone in our hearts to give the light of the knowledge of the glory of God in the face of Christ.[1]

Here then is an apostle, by God's mercy called to a ministry of proclamation, saved by the mercy he now proclaims, turned from persecuting others who had proclaimed the gospel before him. He reminds us, as he puts it, that the life of Jesus was not simply manifested in our flesh in the past – the glory of God seen in the face of one dying then dead but raised by God, and still to be manifested in our flesh. How do we get some sort of sense of God's continuous gracious self-giving to us? Think of Christ's face, he suggests. Recognizing God is somewhat indirect – God is not available to us to grab and snatch at and keep for ourselves, or dish out like doses of medicine brought out from under lock and key. But God's initiative and grace is

---

1 A reading was 2 Corinthians 4.1–6, which appears in the RCL only for the feast day of St Philip and St James, Apostles.

there for us – if we know where to focus our attention – on a face, a particular face.

And this comes from someone acutely sensitive to idolatry: the idolatry of things, of persons, or words, anything that will block off God, or hinder or confuse us in our efforts to respond to God's grace, God's generosity – a grace and a generosity that yet has a face. So keep in mind the question: does this metaphor of Christ's face provide us with the sort of focus we need without tipping us unawares into something like idolatry? Think of how attractive that legend of the true icon has been – the longing expressed in the story of Veronica, the woman who blots the sweaty bleeding face of Christ on his way to execution, so that we can say, 'Here it is, shall we let you see him?' Any 'icons' we may have are meant to be transparent to what lies beyond them, not to be objects we fix on.

And if the face of Christ is to be a face that each of us in our inexhaustible differences can focus on, it's crucial that we shouldn't have too fixed an image of Christ in our imaginations. For think of human faces – 14 different bones, I believe, and at least 100 different muscles just beneath the skin, criss-crossing in extraordinary ways, capable of an astonishing variety of subtle, complex and beautiful movements, some not so beautiful too. The skin is more or less lustrous and transparent, coloured in different ways, and to different depths, as are our eyes and hair.

We spend a lot of time on our face – think of what human beings hang in their ears or pin in their noses or even their lips. We decorate our skin with cosmetics (not just for the stage) and we scar it into patterns or use tattoos. We sometimes wear patches. We take trouble to frame our faces by the way we shape our hair or wear wigs or – some of us – grow moustaches or beards. We wear hats and necklaces, sometimes masks or veils. We wear scent behind our ears and aftershave on our chins.

Some of the faces that intrigue us the most are those of people who have great insight into others, while themselves having faces that can be enigmatic, ambiguous, capable of subtle change, as with some great actors. And faces can terrify us, if deliberately obscured to menace us – wearing a stocking-mask, or kept in shadow while we are mercilessly placed in a blazing light. By contrast, the faces we most want to see are those who share the light with us – light we can bear – those we love and trust and long for, as they love and trust and long for us. Imagine the ways in which we look for one another at railway stations or at bus depots or any other sort of meeting place.

To return to Christ's face from ours – Christ's face can't be meant to menace us. This isn't God in a stocking-mask, but is more likely to be akin to those who have the intriguing or enigmatic or ambiguous qualities of some great actor – someone who may have great insight into others, but who like our friends wants to share the light with us, wants to be seen, to communicate, to show us what we are, what we might be capable of, what we might be capable of becoming. And if it's a face that somehow enables us to glimpse God, it will be a face that will help us to recognize what we're *really* like, not just what we think we're like: help us to face it – to face up to it, as we say – and yet not be crippled by what we see. Paul, you remember, by God's mercy had been called from persecution to proclamation, and somewhere in the experience of this mercy must have been moments of appalled recognition of what he was, what he'd been doing.

And if we were to glance back at an earlier passage (2.10), we'll find him say, 'for if I forgave any thing, to whom I forgave it, for your sakes forgave I it in the person of Christ; lest Satan should get an advantage of us' (KJV). Since we've got into something of a muddle recently over this phrase 'the person of Christ', translators offer another interpretation or translation of the words, 'as the representative of Christ', which may help a bit. The point is that Paul does not suppose he's a kind of literal or physical stand-in for Christ. It's rather that what he does in God's mercy is done in the presence of Christ and under his judgement. But we still need to ask, how do we find the face of Christ? I pointed out that the faces we most want to see will be those we love and trust and long for as they love and trust and long for us. These will be the faces of people quite capable of telling us when we've made idiots of ourselves or have hurt or harmed someone or something but who will go on loving and trusting and longing for us – here is something of the life of Jesus manifest in our bodies.

Let me briefly give you one example, to provoke you to think of your own, drawn not from our present century but from the late thirteenth and early fourteenth, from Dante's life and his *Divine Comedy*. Dante wrote what Dorothy Sayers called a drama of the soul's choice – a drama played out so that we in our turn might learn the taste of heaven, hear of the possibilities of ecstasy, joy and 'the love that moves the sun and other stars'. In the very last part of the *Divine Comedy*, and I've just quoted the last line, 'the love that moves the sun and other stars', Dante tries to write of the Trinity in non-human-face terms, as three spheres of light:

> The first mirrored the next, as though it were,
> Rainbow from Rainbow, and third seemed flame,
> Breathes equally from each of the first pair.

Yet one of these spheres, he writes:

> Seemed in itself, and in its own self-hue,
> Limned with our image; for which cause mine eyes
> were altogether drawn and held thereto.

And whose image is our image? Dante had as a child loved someone he loved as a living woman, and whom he went on loving even after she died, and he became an adult man, married to Gemma, with children of their own. As Charles Williams once wrote, the Beatrice of the *Comedy* is perhaps more like Gemma than even Dante quite knew. Of Beatrice he wrote:

> O say that when she appeared from any direction, then in the hope of her wondrous salutation, there was no enemy left to me; rather there smote into me a flame of charity, which made me forgive any person who had ever injured me; and if at that moment anybody had put a question to

me about anything whatsoever, my answer would have been simply 'Love', with a countenance clothed in humility.[2]

Beatrice had become for him what he could in his turn be for someone else – or we in turn could be for one another – a grace-bearer. That's a somewhat unnerving prospect! It's as though he takes the sort of thing Paul talks about – the life of Jesus manifest in our mortal flesh – entirely seriously, much more seriously than we do. And in the pageant of the sacrament in the *Divine Comedy* Dante has addressed to Beatrice words from the eucharistic liturgy: '*Benedictus qui venis*' – 'Blessed are thou who comest (in the name of the Lord)'. Through seeing her after longing for her eyes and her smile, her sight of him in turn, and the words they exchange, giving and receiving from one another, Dante shows us the mutuality of love, grace, mercy and forgiveness; even the glory of which Paul writes. Dante's words for prayer are 'I in-thee me as thou in meëst thee', while both of them remain very much themselves, and are able to help one another finally to enjoy God – those spheres of the Trinity, one of which is, as Dante put it, 'Limned with our image'. Dante gives us an idea of what Paul talks about when he writes of 'the glory of God in the face of Jesus Christ' and the life of Jesus 'made manifest in our mortal flesh'. And turning it around, I can find in this some encouragement to think that Paul might have been a bit more like Dante than we allow, which is a cheering thought.

In any event, as I've suggested, it's as though we don't take Paul as seriously as maybe Dante did – and to our own hurt. We don't expect to see grace and glory on one another's faces as we meet in the street, and I don't see why we shouldn't. And if we don't, maybe our expectations of how to see one another aren't right, for if we can't enjoy one another, how do we expect to glimpse God's glory in Christ's face? We need to take the risks of paying attention to one another in the way Paul and Dante encourage, and so see God's glory in Christ's face reflected in one another – see it, praise it and love it.

2 Cited in Ann Loades, ed., *Dorothy L. Sayers: Spiritual Writers* (London: SPCK, 1993), 170.

Interlude

19

Why Worship?

My interest in the question, and hence my affirmative response to the request to address it, stems in part from my long-held opinion that there is a good deal wrong with the structure and content of what passes for education in theology.[1] In particular, the neglect of liturgy marks the absence of what should be at the heart of theology – worship – though there is a lot that needs doing to transform the teaching of liturgy also, from what I know of it: too text-bound by half, to put it briefly. On the other hand, if I had known more about the possible difficulties of addressing the question 'why worship?' I might have thought twice about attempting to respond to it, even so. I gather it was Gabriel Daly who suggested it in all its apparent simplicity, and he may well have been more familiar with the difficulties than I was, in my ignorance. I suspect my problems are shared by others facing the same issues. So let us hope I can offer something that may be useful even if it is only to provoke others to offer something more adequate as a response to 'why worship?' It may be helpful to say at the outset that I have come to think that worship is not primarily an activity that can be understood instrumentally – that is, as having its essential point even in such important features of religious life as intercession, confession or forgiveness. Rather, its essential point is adoration. In cultures that privilege utility and instrumentality, the sense of 'adoration' is easily lost. Its near loss was exemplified in the sheer lack of attention to it in the literature I read.

As I see it, while we may all agree that in liturgy we engage

[1] This address was given at Christ Church Cathedral, Dublin (Church of Ireland).

with the very substance of theology – with the very presence of God, however that is mediated to us – and while we may also agree that it is important for some people, some of the time, to engage with the 'how we do it' of liturgy, none of us stop to think about why we worship. Or, at least, if some of us do think through the question, precious little of it gets into print. If one acknowledges the importance of the question, one may well find that a near total blank may be the sum of what is to be found in a library. So what is going on here, or not going on, and does it matter? Now of course one might say that we do not need to think about the question, and to publish what we think. Worship just is part of being human, it is what human beings get up to from time to time. Can we stop there? Suppose we move beyond that deceptively simple descriptive comment and attempt to think what worship may mean in respect of human flourishing. We might want to add that it is necessary that human beings engage in worship, because otherwise they get somewhat atrophied, stunted, cut short – or that is the claim of some. So we are not dealing here with an aspect of what it is to be human that we need to outgrow (one possible view) – or so we hope – but with something so integral to the fruition and fulfilment of what it is not just to exist as a human being, that it is integral to becoming a fully human person, or, put more strongly, become a normal human person.[2]

Thus already, in trying to sketch a very minimal response to the question, which we might think was sufficient to put a stop to thinking about it so we can get on with the 'what' and the 'how' of it, we may find ourselves led to make certain kinds of claims: claims that need attention. If worship is as essential as we may suppose it is to the possibility of our becoming fully and normally human persons, we can be sure that there is a lot that can go badly wrong with worship too. So we really do need to think about 'why worship?' and what is involved here. How are we to set about it? As I have indicated, there is not much help to be found in publications. Try looking up 'worship' in theological dictionaries or in catechisms. The most

2 See Aidan Kavanagh on 'Liturgy and normality' in his *On Liturgical Theology* (New York: Pueblo, 1992), 151–76.

on offer is likely to be a cross-reference to 'adoration', and on looking there we find the same lack of elucidation. In a way, that is a relief, but also a challenge, for it puts the responsibility for thinking the question back where it belongs – not with authorities, but with us, we who worship, even if we do not initially think ourselves up to it. The point is suitably made for us by Annie Dillard:

> I know only enough of God to want to worship him, by any means ready to hand. There is an anomalous specificity to all our experience in space, a scandal of particularity, by which God burgeons up or showers down into the shabbiest of occasions, and leaves his creation's dealings with him in the hands of purblind and clumsy amateurs. This is all we are and all we ever were; *God kann nicht anders.* This process in time is history; in space, at such shocking random, it is a mystery.
>
> A blur of romance clings to our notions of 'publicans', 'sinners', 'the poor', 'the people in the marketplace', 'our neighbors', as though of course God should reveal himself, if at all, to these simple people, these Sunday school watercolor figures, who are so purely themselves in their tattered robes, who are single in themselves, while we now are various, complex and full at heart. We are busy. So, I see now, were they. Who shall ascend into the hill of the Lord? Or who shall stand in his holy place? There is no one but us. There is no one to send, nor a clean hand, nor a pure heart on the face of the earth, nor in the earth, but only us, a generation comforting ourselves with the notion that we have come at an awkward time, that our innocent fathers are all dead – as if innocence had ever been – and our children busy and troubled, and we ourselves unfit, not yet ready, having each of us chosen wrongly, made a false start, failed, yielded to impulse and the tangled comfort of pleasures, and grown exhausted, unable to seek the thread, weak, and involved. But there is no one but us. There never has been.[3]

---

3 Annie Dillard, *Holy the Firm* (London: Harper & Row, 1988), 55–7.

So how to set about it, once we recognize that 'why worship?' is a question for all of us? What we are looking for can be modestly put, I think, in terms of possible responses to our question, not definitive 'answers'. So what we need to do is to hunt and seek for 'reminders', things we all know about in one way or another, and then put those reminders together. So my task at this point is to attempt to make explicit what seems to be implicit, to remind us of what in some sense we already know, and put those reminders together for our consideration, disagreement or agreement.

One reminder to begin with. I take it that 'why worship?' presupposes 'God'. This is not the time or the place to argue for theological realism or non-realism. I simply think that 'why worship?' in our context presupposes God 'other' than us: not us, not our world, not for grabs, not for control, unnameable, unsafe, beyond our idolatries (including what we take to be 'real' even of God in godself); beyond our self-intoxication, self-preoccupation, delusions, needs and harms, both necessary and unsayable. Second reminder: Christian human beings engage with this God, or seek to do so, because they believe that this God seeks them. See John 4.23 and Christ's conversation with the Samaritan woman or Genesis 3.9 and God's hunt for and call to his earth creatures in the garden. And Christian human beings rely on God's marvellous ambiguity – not just his flesh-making but his flesh-taking. That means that the unsayable God becomes Word made flesh – to some degree sayable in his seeking. Some reason for worship, surely. Our response to God is important. Take as illustration Gregory Dix on God's sunlike shining on us:

> Tranquilly, unendingly from the depths of His own being His love plays upon us and He swings us unceasingly on our life's way and holds us and draws us to Him. And we draw Him to us. However slight by comparison with the sun's vast attraction upon the earth, the earth's little pull upon the sun is real; it does happen.[4]

---

4 Quoted in Simon Bailey, *A Tactful God: Gregory Dix, Priest, Monk and Scholar* (London: Gracewing, 1995), 83–4.

'Why worship?' – to respond! Hence then the Orthodox Alexander Schmemann writing of the rediscovery of worship as 'the life of the Church, the public act ... which embraces, expresses, inspires and defines the whole church, her whole essential nature, her whole life'.[5]

Third reminder: we could so easily mishear Annie Dillard's plea for our responsibility – 'there is no one but us. There never has been.' But what about 'angels and archangels and all the company of heaven'? Part of the answer to 'why worship?' is 'to join in', the feasting, the party-time, where Christ is the 'host'. 'Why worship?' is at least like 'why "party"?', in that party and worship are their own point. They serve no purposes extrinsic to themselves, but if we want to spell it out, try the following: conviviality – the capacity to live together, rivalry and tensions over and done with; companionship – the capacity to share food generously with one another; and general exuberance and *joie de vivre*. Read the second-century book of Jubilees and the canonical book of Revelation. Both constitute invitations to join in, whether in hilarity or in solemnity, maybe both. We may not give 'angels and archangels' much attention most of the time, but the phrase represents matters to which we must pay attention, not simply to make sense of Scripture and tradition but because we want to make sense of our question, 'why worship?' We might try Karl Barth on 'God's heavenly kingdom and His servants the angels' in his *Church Dogmatics* (III:3 section 51) for a twentieth-century Calvinist theological view. More briefly, we can learn from Annie Dillard on Isaiah 6 from which we take the Sanctus of the liturgy:

> Angels, I read, belong to nine different orders. Seraphs are the highest: they are aflame with love for God, and stand closer to him than the others. Seraphs love God; cherubs, who are second, possess perfect knowledge of him. So love is greater than knowledge: how could I have forgotten? The seraphs are born of a stream of fire issuing from under God's throne. They are, according to Dionysius the Areopagite,

---

5 Alexander Schmemann, *Introduction to Liturgical Theology* (New York: SVS Press, 1986), 18.

'all wings', having, as Isaiah noted, six wings apiece, two of which they fold over their eyes. Moving perpetually toward God, they perpetually praise him, crying Holy, Holy, Holy … but, according to some rabbinic writings, they can sing only the first 'Holy' before the intensity of their love ignites them again and dissolves them again, perpetually, into flames.[6]

Our response in worship, that is, takes place in harmony with theirs.

Also, it is arguable that we make a distinctive contribution to the praise of creation offered to God, as C. S. Lewis remarked in *Letters to Malcolm*, in the course of expounding 'Bless the Body'. But for the body, Lewis claimed, part of the whole realm of God's glory would go unpraised. Angels, for instance, as pure intelligences, may understand colours and tastes, but, Lewis asked, 'have they retinas or palates?' Some of the beauties of nature are shared with human beings alone. 'That may be one of the reasons why we were made – and why the resurrection of the body is an important doctrine.'[7] As Lewis himself well knew, no more unequivocal way of putting that can be found than in the third part of Dante's *Divine Comedy*.[8] Here Solomon, embodiment of royal wisdom and poet of the Song of Songs, is to be found in the company of the Church's greatest teachers, delivering the doctrine of the resurrection in terms of 'holy and glorious flesh' – presumably something like Christ's own risen and ascended humanity.

And that remark of Lewis' connects with another dimension of worship. We can take 'the company of heaven' to be a reference to the *communio sanctorum*, the 'communion of saints' or the company of the sanctified, who share the conviviality, the companionship, the exuberance and the *joie de vivre* of a repossessed paradise. Faithful departed – yes; dead – no, and encompassing more than we can presently imagine. For a vision of an all-inclusive humanity, we may read Flannery O'Connor's wonderful short story 'Revelation' in her collection

---

6 Dillard, *Holy the Firm*, 45.

7 C. S. Lewis, *Letters to Malcolm* (London: Penguin, 1964), 29.

8 Dante, *Paradise*, Canto 14.

Everything That Rises Must Converge[9] and the excellent book
on the communion of saints, Elizabeth A. Johnson's *Friends of
God and Prophets.*[10]

My main point here is that without some allusions to angels
and archangels and all the company of heaven we neglect
the context of worship and the company and so we will miss
part of the point. And so to my fourth reminder, which is
that the point is to be caught up as these other creatures are
into God's trinitarian life – God's self-understanding, God's
sanctity, God's exchange of love, God's generosity, stretching
us beyond what we think to be our capacities. God is beyond
our idolatries, including our idolatries of speech, but because
God seeks and calls, we in response learn to stammer 'Trinity',
learning this in ceremonies in which we invoke 'God, Christ,
Spirit'. It is to this God that worship may lure us, not merely
focusing us on the divine but gracing us into divine being. Let
us be grateful for help where we find it, too. The most moving
invocation of the Trinity I personally have ever heard was in
a performance of liturgical music by The Sixteen in Durham
Cathedral which concluded with a piece of sixteenth-century
polyphony by John Sheppard. This was polyphony using a
deceptively simple text: 'Free us, save us, defend us, O blessed
Trinity': *Libera nos, salva nos, justifica nos O beata Trinitas.*

Our attempts to stammer can be such that we need to hope
that heaven enjoys a joke, given our pomposity on the one hand
and the shabby, shoddy, chaotic, incoherent 'kitsch' we can go
in for on the other, at least sometimes, in our efforts to respond,
and to join in. Take, for instance, David Hare's the Revd Lionel
Espy in his play *Racing Demon*. His view is that much of what
passes for religion is nonsense. His argument is that people
hole up in church and tell God how wonderful he is. 'God,
you're so terrific. No, really. Terrific.' Though the more people
doing this might be regarded by some as 'thriving', Lionel's

9 Flannery O'Connor, *Everything That Rises Must Converge* (London: Faber, 1966), 191–218.

10 Elizabeth A. Johnson, *Friends of God and Prophets* (London: SCM Press, 1998).

question remains, 'Where does [it] get you?'[11] The response to that is not that it must always be awful, but to pray to do it better: 'Cleanse the thoughts of our hearts by the inspiration of thy Holy Spirit, that we may perfectly love thee and worthily magnify thy holy name' represents an aspiration that is capable of fulfilment. And that may be assisted by attending to our fifth reminder, which is about *koinonia hagion*, making the common holy, and making the holy common. For example, consider part of Thomas Traherne's poem, 'The World':

> The sun, that gilded all the bordering woods,
> Shone from the sky
> To beautify
> My earthly and my heavenly goods;
> Exalted in his throne on high,
> He shed his beams
> In golden streams
> That did illustrate all the sky;
> Those floods of light, his mantle rays,
> Did fill the glitt'ring ways,
>
> While that unsufferable piercing eye
> The ground did glorify.
> The choicest colours, yellow, green and blue
> Did all this court
> In comely sort
> With mixed varieties bestrew;
> Like gold with emeralds between;
> As if my God
> From his abode
> By these intended to be seen.
> And so He was.[12]

Or take Gregory Dix's perceptions:

---

11 David Hare, *Racing Demon* (London: Faber, 1990), 64.

12 Thomas Traherne, 'The World', in *Poems of Felicity* (Oxford: Clarendon Press, 1910), 89–90.

Anyone who has had one little glimpse of the corner of the glory of God, or the very outskirts of His ways, they will know that God is in Himself, for His own sake, lovely. It is very difficult to realise that God would have deserved all love if there had never been any creatures. I think the first time I realised that was when I was about twenty-five years of age and I walked up to a big hill in Gloucester, in England. It was a famous hill. You walk up a long dusty hill from the Gloucester side, you can't see anything except about two yards of dusty road in front of you. You come out on the top of the hill and there is perhaps the loveliest, softest landscape in the whole of England. Spread out to view is the whole valley with Gloucester Cathedral tower standing up in the middle, and this gorgeous view stretching right away to the mountains. I suddenly realised it wasn't anything in me, it was something in that view which had wrenched the admiration out of me. And that it had been just as lovely while I had been coming up the hill and couldn't see it at all. God is like that, for His own sake, in His own self, apart from what He does for me, lovely.[13]

Both Traherne and Dix illustrate what Karl Rahner says of worship, where he writes of it as an explicit celebration of the divine depth of ordinary life.[14] And I see no necessity whatsoever to suppose that, in urban and 'high-tech' contexts which superficially at least seem to be so largely constituted by human imagination and the powers of human making, this sense of the celebration of the divine depth of ordinary life must inevitably be lost. On the contrary, human achievement can positively give us clues to that 'divine depth' if referred to its primary creative source, safeguarding human beings from self-destructive pride. It is precisely the capacity to imagine and to make things of all levels of sophistication that can make us more rather than less alert to divine creativity and able to praise God for it. Finding the divine depth of ordinary

---

13 Recounted in Bailey, *A Tactful God*, 24.
14 See Karl Rahner, 'On the Theology of Worship' in his *Theological Investigations* 19 (London: Darton, Longman and Todd, 1984), 141–9.

life is also to be associated with certain ways of patterning life by sacramental practices, and developing certain strengths (virtues) associated with that patterning, which may come to mark the lives of those to be transformed and finally trans-figured by God – faith, fortitude, charity, justice, prudence, temperance and hope. There are many 'patterns', no doubt, but that they are vital to practise will be seen in the capacity to praise God for the splendours of redemption even in the most appalling circumstances. So let me now turn to this dimension of our 'why worship?' question too.

The Hebrew Scriptures are drenched with the praise of God, with the 'blessing' of God's name, the acknowledgement of God as God associated with the habit of thanksgiving.[15] One example of this is to be found in 1 Chronicles 29.10–11 on the lips of King David: 'Blessed art thou, O LORD, the God of Israel our father, for ever and ever. Thine, O LORD, is the greatness, and the power, and the glory, and the victory, and the majesty; for all that is in the heavens and in the earth is thine, thine is the kingdom, O LORD, and thou art exalted as head above all.' The assembly makes three responses at this point. The people bow their heads; they prostrate them-selves; and they make sacrifices. We glimpse in and through the text the words and behaviour of those who have learned, or are in the process of learning, to praise God for nothing, simply because God is God. Our sixth reminder, then, is that we worship God in order to be able to go on doing so, no matter what. Those who have so learned to praise God con-tinue to praise God in extremity. Two examples are the echoes of Psalm 22 on the lips of St Mark's Gospel's crucified Jesus and, from a very different world, Yaffa Eliah's account of 'the first Hanukkah Light in Bergen Belsen'.[16] The prisoners con-structed a makeshift hanukkiah from a wooden clog, strings and shoe polish to serve as oil. Living skeletons surrounded by the bodies of the dead, including those of their own fami-

15 See Stephen B. Dawes, '"Bless the Lord": An Invitation to Affirm the Living God', *The Expository Times* 106:10 (1995), 293–6.

16 See Michael Downey, 'Worship between the Holocausts', *Theology Today* 43 (1986), 75–87.

lies and loved ones, they nonetheless assembled to kindle the lights. The rabbi might well hesitate – but he proceeded with the third blessing, in which God, addressed as Lord and King of the universe, is blessed for keeping, preserving and enabling the covenant people to reach this season. If God has a people still living, their faces expressing faith, devotion and concentration, though death stares at them from every corner, then the prayer is justified. So to put our point again, in the worship of God we align ourselves with God's defeat of evil, overheard in Christ's words from the cross, seen at Hanukkah in a death camp, and manifest in Christ's risen and glorified humanity which embraces the humanity not only of the victims but of those who betray and destroy others. So the worship of God requires taking seriously not only the beauties of the world but its horrors too. There is nothing anaemic about the 'guts and grief' that will be required, or the realization that the worship of God will therefore necessarily involve prayer for the 'enemy', intercession for the 'hangers-on' of death and the descents into hell that they make possible. As with the worship of God, however, Christians do not suppose themselves to be required to tackle this on their own. Least of all here are the worshippers of God thrust back on their own resources. Therefore 'why worship?' also requires a political response of a kind. Hence to our seventh reminder.

That we are involved in a 'political' activity is implicit in the Kyrie, the Sanctus, the creeds, and other central liturgical texts. To recite these texts is to declare loyalty, to put the 'lords' of this world, even the very best of them, in their places. And although almost a commonplace, it deserves repeating that the worship of God undertaken by the Church is not for the Church's sake, but for the world's sake: for the energy, the capacity for politics, the life of the 'city', to go on with it, not bound by the worst, but determined, courageous and hopeful enough to make and share the best. Perhaps nothing could be more significant of the fact that worship is a political act than prayer for the enemy, for the lords of horror, intercession for them, excruciating though that may be. Almost equally painful may be prayer for the capacity to forgive as we are forgiven.

With the capacity to pray for the enemy, perhaps we have the most signal marks of God's service of humankind which initiates and sustains human service of God. Joseph embraced his brothers, and they him, eventually. Jacob is reconciled with Esau: 'to see your face is like seeing the face of God, with such favour have you received me' (Genesis 33.10).

There may be other signs that distinguish those who worship God, or so we may suppose – and I have left this until the last so that we do not begin by thinking that 'why worship?' has something to do with 'usefulness' to us. We may, however, finally permit ourselves to think that habits of worship and praise of God may foster habits of praise of one another; delight in God – delight in one another; bless God's name – bless one another's distinctive being; grace one another into life as God graces us; learn the habits of thanks; acknowledge and live out the intradependence of 'Abide in me, as I in you' (John 15.4). I do not think it is accidental that it is a philosopher who is also a Christian who can say in his book *Dependent Rational Animals*: 'I can be said truly to know who and what I am, only because there are others who can be said truly to know who and what I am.'[17] Worship has to do with abiding, trusting, securing the bonds of covenant. We might even grow up enough to learn to be penitent; to learn to travel light; to mark time differently; to clear space; to concentrate, attend, persevere, wait, listen in stillness and silence.

All that said, let us return to the most important direction of 'why worship?' In her book *Worship*,[18] Evelyn Underhill observed that worship 'always means the priority of God', but that 'we in our worshipping action are compelled to move within the devotional sphere, with all its symbolic furniture, its archaic survivals, its pitfalls, its risks of sentimentalism, herd-suggestion, and disguised self-regard'. God remains over against all this in utter freedom and distinctiveness. Forget the contrast between God and ourselves, and we shall never understand the religious scene. 'There is no department of

---

17 Alasdair MacIntyre, *Dependent Rational Animals* (London: Duckworth, 2000), 95.

18 Evelyn Underhill, *Worship* (London: Nisbet, 1936).

life which asks from those who study it so much humble sympathy, such a wide, genial, unfastidious spirit, or so constant a remembrance of our own limitations as this.' Whatever the hazards, she believed, as may we, that the divine invitation to worship and our response to it is the means by which we move through this life.[19] Moreover, it is undertaken 'to achieve that transfiguration of the whole created universe, that shining forth of the splendour of the Holy, in which the aim of worship shall be fulfilled' – the last words of her book![20] That seems indeed to be a very tall order for us, but it is at least 'orthodox' in the sense of 'true opinion' to be a sufficient concluding response to 'why worship?'

---

19 Underhill, *Worship*, 6.
20 Underhill, *Worship*, 343.

20

Word and Sacrament

I have three overall concerns in these reflections which attempt to do no more than map out a position.[1]

I am attempting to rediscover a way of thinking, imagining 'Christianly', something of the character of God's relation to the world (whatever there is), a way that we on the whole neglect, and that to our cost. The three concerns that mark this hoped-for rediscovery are sacramentality, the importance of liturgy and preaching, and the significance of the arts for theology. One preliminary comment: we have become accustomed to think about God's relationship to creation in terms of the science–religion debate. My reflections deliberately eschew concern with that debate with all its limitations, notwithstanding its undoubted importance.

I begin by mapping my position by introducing some important vocabulary, and 'sacramental' is the obvious place to start, very broadly construed. For my purposes and at this point, experiencing the world as sacramental is to experience it as mediating divine presence to us, a presence richly personal which initiates such mediation. We need of course to avoid a particular cluster of errors in association with a sacramental way of experiencing the world, since we are always in danger of such forms of idolatry and superstition manifesting themselves in attributing to things power or powers they do not, should not, or cannot have. We can do something to avoid these errors if we hold sacramental in some tension with 'spiritual', as in

---

1 This address was given at Australian Catholic University, Brisbane.

'spiritual sacramentality' or 'sacramental spirituality' perhaps, making one adjectival to the other. To refer to the spiritual here is not to be limited to self-preoccupation, valuable though that may be in the initial stages of sorting oneself out/engaging with another in that process of sorting out. It is to develop a sense of divine presence as transcendent to us, with the word 'spiritual' as a marker of such transcendence. We need, however, to return to our 'sacramental' insistence that it is matter and flesh that mediate the spiritual, the transcendent, to avoid another cluster of errors. Overemphasis on the spiritual can precipitate us into a kind of gnostic disease, the symptoms of which are that we find ourselves nauseated by or disgusted with the context in which we find ourselves. (Waugh's title phrase *Vile Bodies* or Sartre's *La Nausée* make the point.) To affirm God as creator is to claim in specifically Christian terms that God is with us, for us, present to us, immanent in creation as well as transcendent to it, and that we are made for and of this world. To use words like sacrament/al, spirit/ual, transcendence and immanence, then, is deliberately to foster a sense of tension about meaning. Such a sense of tension may well be intrinsic to a religion that has incarnation at its heart, a meal (of a kind) as a central act of worship, and the promise of bodily, emotional and intellectual fulfilment in the doctrine of resurrection. Where the sense of tension may be slackening, it can be regenerated by rethinking some of the possible links: sacrament-and-transcendence, spirituality-and-immanence, for instance – whatever may provoke the determination to avoid superstition on the one hand and fear of and the attempt to fly from God's world on the other.

It is obvious that sacramentality is being thought of here in connection with the doctrine of creation rather than the doctrine of redemption. My second main concern with liturgy and preaching will relate sacramentality to specific sacraments of redemption. My third concern, with the arts, relates to both the doctrines just mentioned, and is a connecting thread throughout these reflections. More particularly, one fundamental underlying connection in what I am attempting to say is that being Christian is not simply to be a person who subscribes to a set of beliefs or facts, though Christianity most certainly requires attention to what is true or false, to what is or is not the case, or might or might not be the case. Being Christian engages imagination and emotion, energy and passion, not as 'extra' to belief but as integral, central to it. And we might inhabit our tradition with greater ease if we learned to give emotion and imagination greater weight as we try to find our way about in it. For if these dimensions of our lives are not engaged, can we effectively and seriously believe? It is at least arguable that intellectual impoverishment and neglect of these other dimensions of ourselves are profoundly connected to one another. The arts have their own integrity and do not exist to serve the interests of theology, but theology may not flourish in all its dimensions unless those aspects of being human explored and celebrated by the arts are also the focus of our attention. Moreover, theology need not assume a position of epistemological primacy or superiority here. In other words, theology needs to learn from the perception of artists about dimensions of reality that otherwise we may fail to notice and from which we sorely need to learn.

2

We may thus far agree that sacramentality, very broadly construed, reflects the confidence that anything in principle may or might mediate God to us. This seems to follow from the crucifixion as a central symbol of Christian tradition. In other words, if the horrors of judicial execution can be the means of divine revelation so might the boring, the banal, the squalid, the morally problematic. The paintings of Rouault may be particularly illuminating here. And as I have already said, the particularities arising from the incarnation, the 'events' of salvation and the specific sacraments of the Christian tradition will receive at least some attention when we turn to considering the importance of Christian liturgy. If it needs reinforcement, I hope that the importance of starting from 'creation' rather than from 'redemption' may be clear by the end of what I want to say, if it is not clear already. And to repeat something said already in a different way in connection with being wary of idolatry and superstition, it is clear that it is God who initiates such mediation of divine presence as may be possible to us and for us. The mediation of God can never be a matter of our deliberately attempting to manipulate flesh, matter, bodyliness, spirit or word to 'cause' divine presence, not even in the most authoritative form we can devise in liturgy. A human selfmaking of divine presence is a contradiction in terms and a thoroughly futile endeavour. To speak of the mediation of the divine presence, transfiguring our world, or some part or aspect of it, is rather a matter of allowing for the possibility of it, of relishing it wherever it just so happens to be around, to surface perhaps, to be not merely unmistakably but perhaps even ambiguously just 'there'. Another way of thinking sacramentally from the doctrine of creation is to note that Christianity is marked by catholicity – that is, by concern with and directed to the whole. In this case, this means the context in which we are to be found and in which we find ourselves, and which is not ours, because it belongs to, and is derived from, another. This could in principle have important consequences for our willingness to learn from non-Christian religious traditions in a generous way.

Sacramentality and catholicity, then, are closely connected to belief in creation, creativity, whether divine or human. Where we do not pay attention to appropriate threads of connection, Christians and non-Christians will scavenge for them wherever they can find them, for instance in what passes for Celtic spirituality, or Gaia or god/dess spirituality. Human creatures turn readily to the natural for a sense of the divine, which they may well associate with the unviolated and the unspoiled, though what appears to be natural (see landscape and landscape painting) is at least sometimes or to some extent a matter of creative contrivance. And if not to the natural, human creatures turn to the realm of human making, of *poiesis*. Poetry, the peculiarly human resources of richly metaphorical language in all its dimensions, is undeniably important in the purely gratuitous mediation of the sense of divine presence. Perhaps initially we think of its importance in relation to prayers, hymns and sermons as well as in 'poetry' in the ordinary sense. But there are other means of mediation by 'word', such as drama and in combination with the less or only tangentially verbal, such as music, cinema, soaps, film and photography, advertising. Dance too may integrate word with movement and music, and not only in musicals; and we can certainly talk about glass-making, gardening, engineering, design, fashion and clothing, sculpture, metalwork, embroidering, food, buildings, public space and the use we make of it. Our social and political lives are themselves constituted by these manifold forms of creativity, to which we might nowadays add the creativity of the manager and the entrepreneur and the 'fixer'. Sacramental spirituality has profound and far-reaching ethical and social connotations, for it is expressed and mediated through who and what we are, in interconnection with all else/others. Words like conviviality (living with others), companionship (eating with others) and sheer *joie de vivre* may capture some of it. Picking up a thread from an earlier paragraph, we might note that if we overemphasize transcendence we can construe it all too easily as absence – the world stripped bare of divine presence, the city-spaces of the liberal-rational state. In such a context, religion may be thrust at best into the realm of the 'private' and the comfort-zone/blanket-sucking aspects or needs even of adult lives, and manifest in religious trinketry, tat and fussiness. Much discrimination is needed here, but the main point of what I am saying represents resistance to the trivialization of the sacramental. Such resistance may well require a certain sort of willingness to live dangerously and with a sort of cheerful and invigorating panache in the world, about which we might learn much from the entrepreneurs. For a renewed sacramentality we probably need a new list of fruits of the spirit relevant to our shared lives together, not to displace the familiar scriptural lists but to represent more adequately the gifts needed for living in our risky, mistake-ridden, very complex world.

One point to which we need to give explicit attention is that we should be alert to the dangers of being too high-minded about 'human making' when we want to attend to sacramentality and catholicity. One of the gifts of a priest such as Stewart Headlam to the Church at large was the reminder that Christian faith is not to be identified with discomfort about vulgarity.[2] Yes, it is tremendous fun and exhibits guts and gusto, but will it last, and is it in good taste or is it kitsch? And in the Church of England, will it get past the Fabric Commission? What sort of criteria are these, and why should they be important to us? Some of our criteria may be class-based (or racially biased or gender-biased, and we may become appropriately sensitive to these). We might be less worried about the apparently vulgar if we appreciated more readily that the sacramental may rightly be associated with the temporary, the throwaway. Given the utterances made on occasion about faith as a pilgrimage, a journey, 'this transitory life' and so on, there is no necessary association of divine presence with the permanent, the continuously present, so that ecclesiastical buildings over time come to resemble left luggage offices that may never be cleared. (Such clearing need not imply destruction, only storage until a different age of appreciation, perhaps.) Divine presence may very properly be associated with the fleeting, the contingent, here today and gone tomorrow, with travelling light. After all, most of the material signs of specific sacraments are fluid, or consumable, transient, except in their immediate or longer-term effects on the persons concerned, themselves the pilgrims. (Think here of bread, wine, oil, water, candle flames, hands in blessing.) And in societies in which there is a near obsession with recording everything, whether by film or tape or whatever, especially when recording is followed by analysis, dissection and the countable, we need to destabilize the sense that only these things are real, and that by 'real' we do not mean what can be frozen or fixed for our attention, and indeed cannot be, if divine presence is somehow to be manifested in relation to human persons.

---

2 John R. Orens, *Stewart Headlam's Radical Anglicanism: The Mass, Masses, and Music Halls* (Chicago, IL: University of Illinois Press, 1979).

Finally for this section, we might bear 'tradition' in mind in relation to sacramentality, the creative and the catholic. It is of crucial importance that we have a sense of inhabiting the past that is both handed on to us and to which and for which we are responsible in our turn. To illustrate the importance of tradition we have only to look at what happens to a particular people when a stronger group systematically destroys their past as part of a strategy for destroying them. Tradition, therefore, is not 'the dead hand of the past' that will mummify us too if we let it, but a life-giving source of vitality. How human beings live with one another and all else is fascinating and complex and exhibits an almost inexhaustible range of possibilities, even looking no further than Christianity itself. We might look, for instance, at the lives of the 'saints', from child-bearing women to warriors representing an astonishing range of imaginative possibilities. Tradition is of its essence creative and innovative, with all the graces of intelligence and skill we can muster. Certainly we must learn from the past, if only to generate critical dissonance with the present, to open up new vistas and walkways, generate new insights, negotiate dead-ends, endure experiences of profound alienation, and live with changing criteria. The past, however, neither does nor should control the present or the future, and at one level we are all perfectly familiar with this. If we were not, we would not be able to say the Apostles' Creed, let alone the Nicene, at the appropriate points in our liturgies. In the case of the former creed, attention to what can be known about its history reveals the introduction of innovative clauses into the 'original' ground-creeds so far as we can discover them, and a long and fascinating history of interpretation of those clauses in varying social and political contexts. In the case of the Nicene Creed its theologically innovative language and commitments reveal a particularly contentious history. We might then say that traditionalists are themselves spirit-bearers, or that they are pneumatophoric, to use a word from Orthodoxy, though this is hardly to be claimed for oneself, but attributed by others, and to self-with-others. If being pneumatophoric sounds too puzzling out of the Orthodox context, then 'graced presence/s' may serve instead.

Grace has an unmistakable bodily resonance, after all: to say 'that was a graceful gesture' is not simply to make a remark about how someone moves (though Canova's statue of the 'Three Graces' reminds us of the physical beauty of grace), but it is associated with movement of some kind. We might then think of sacramentality in terms of 'inner conviction of visible or experienceable grace or graces' to be evident in lively and committed tradition bearers.

That, so far, is a very broad-brush mapping of some of the things we might like to think about, and at this point it may be helpful to have a particular example of reflection on and expression of the richly textured world in which we find ourselves. Kathleen Raine's 'Word made Flesh' is a meditation on the way in which divine Word has taken 'flesh' not only in the incarnation but in the extraordinary order and beauty of the world we see around us: a Word 'whose breath is the world-circling atmosphere', 'turns the wind', 'articulates the bird that speeds upon the air', blazes in the sun, makes music with stars and dawn, can be traced in light on water and in colours of cloud, is inscribed on mountain ranges, fires the sun, unfolds lilies, spirals in leaves and shells, and more in a 'myriadfold vision of the world':

> Statement of mystery, how shall we name
> a spirit clothed in world, a world made man?[3]

In this connection I find valuable Annie Dillard's comment that 'material complexity is the truth of the world, even the workable world of idea, and must be the truth of the art object which would imitate, order and penetrate that world: complexity, and contradiction, and repetition, diversity, energy and largesse. I am as attracted to purity as the next guy. But it must not happen here.'[4] The final poem to which I shall refer also plays on the notion of 'largesse'.

---

3 Find the full poem in David Brown and David Fuller, eds, *Signs of Grace: The Sacraments in Poetry and Prose* (London: Cassell, 1995), 4–5.

4 Annie Dillard, *Living by Fiction* (San Francisco, CA: Harper, 1982), 172.

3

In this section we move to consideration of the connections we need to make between the sacramental, the catholic, the creative and the importance of liturgy. This is to narrow my focus to what we may think is the proper area of the sacramental, if indeed we think of it at all. There may be both good and bad reasons for this state of affairs, which I do not intend to explore. What does seem to matter at this junction is that we do not seem on the whole, and with rare exceptions, to be engaging theologically, religiously, with what it is to be the kind of beings who offer worship to God, respond to God's unimaginable generosity not only with gratitude but with delight. I do not think that such engagement is reducible to learning about rubrics, or to who wears what and why, or to how many sacraments there are, or might be. Any or all of these matters may be important, but are not at the heart of it. For what we somehow need to engage with, focus on, reflect on, articulate, is that our 'ceremonious' activity enables us to 'say' God. However simple it is, however pared down, whatever the balance of the verbal or non-verbal (and giving the highest importance to preaching), it is because we do these things, sing these hymns, repeat these words, that we are able to say 'God, Christ, Spirit' together, to learn to live Trinitarianly. We can give no sense to our doctrines unless we engage in these practices.[5] The doctrines of creation and redemption need to be explored in Trinitarian terms, and there is no space here to do so. My point is fundamentally about liturgy as a sort of 'performance' which is essential to the possibility of learning certain beliefs. And since my initial emphasis has been on creation and sacramentality, and I have turned now to specifically Christian liturgy and the integrity of word and particular sacrament in that liturgy, we should perhaps bear in mind that creation and redemption are doctrines systematically to be connected. Most minimally: 'I set my bow in the cloud and it shall be a sign of the covenant'.

---

5 Fergus Kerr, 'The Trinity and Christian Life', *Priests and People* 7 (1993), 233–7.

Holding the two together is another area of fruitful tension, and there are others. If we cannot endure or enjoy such tension and find it creative we find ourselves limited to one aspect of it or another: being fallen/sanctified; the necessity of redemption/ the possibility of transformation; justification/holiness; word and obedience/sacrament and participation. Particularly we need to attend to meanings of baptism and Eucharist, and their transformations of those most elementary acts of washing and feeding without which no child can survive; and the connections of both with penitence and forgiveness without which we cannot go on. I shall return to this when turning to the responsibilities of the preacher. My view is that it is in liturgy that we learn and are lured to God in certain specific ways, so if liturgy is bungled it is serious, and its consideration is far too important to be left to the periphery of theology, or to training for ordained ministry.

I want to emphasize my point about the importance of preaching by associating it with the traditional categories of 'corporal' and 'spiritual' works of mercy. The former are those that may be associated with the great parable of Matthew 25.31–46 and with chapters 1—2 of Tobit, and the bodily mercies of food and drink to the needy, clothing and shelter to the destitute, visits to the sick and imprisoned, and providing burial for the dead, any or all of which may require much sensitivity and creativity. Or consider Isaiah 58.6–9: 'Is not this the fast that I choose ...?' – sharing with the hungry, housing the poor, breaking the yoke of oppression.

Spiritual works of mercy are to convert the sinner, to instruct the ignorant, counsel the doubtful, comfort the sorrowful, learn to bear wrongs patiently, forgive injuries and to pray for the living and the dead. People cannot learn these things unless they are taught, and there are more ways of teaching them than simply saying something, but it must be among the responsibilities of a preacher to teach them, to begin the process of learning and practising them. People need to hear of God's unimaginable generosity to them if they are to express their delight in God in return, and if they do not hear it from preaching in the context of liturgy, where else will they?

If we need to emphasize any one responsibility of the preacher at the present time, we might focus especially on the problematic matter of forgiveness, of how we open up the future not being defined either by the wrong we do or the wrong done to us. Hannah Arendt has claimed that the discoverer of the role of forgiveness in human affairs was Jesus of Nazareth – at least the form of it that simply dismisses what we have done unknowingly and releases us from it. 'Only through this constant mutual release from what they can do can men remain free agents, only by constant willingness to change their minds and start again can they be trusted with so great a power as that to begin something new.' The most powerful lived experience of that power for Arendt has to do with 'natality' and the words 'a child has been born unto us', and the theme of nativity and promise could be illuminating here.[6] Without pursuing that theme, we acknowledge simply that we may open up the possibility of forgiveness by penitence, and the resource of the language of Psalm 130 for instance needs to be kept alive in us and for us, as in Thomas Campion's translation:

> Out of my soul's depth to thee my cries have sounded:
> Let thine ears my plaints receive, on just fear grounded.
> Lord, should'st thou weigh our faults, who's not confounded?
> But with grace thou censur'st thine when they have erred,
> therefore shall thy blessed name be loved and feared.
> E'en to thy throne my thoughts and eyes are reared.
> Thee alone my hopes attend, on thee relying:
> In thy sacred word I'll trust, to thee fast flying,
> long ere the watch shall break, the morn descrying.
>
> In the mercies of our God who live secured,
> May of full redemption rest in him assured,
> their sin-sick souls by him shall be recured.[7]

---

6 Hannah Arendt, *The Human Condition* (New York: Doubleday, 1958), 212–13.

7 Quoted from Brown and Fuller, eds, *Signs of Grace*, 135.

The sheer incomprehension of forgiveness may well be one of the marks of a deeply secularized society, which may be detected, for instance, in audience reactions to Marlowe's treatment of Faust compared to that of Goethe (whether or not Goethe ever thought his version would actually be performed may affect the manner in which he wrote it, but not the fact that he deals with Faust as a character in the way that he finally does). The reactions of an audience may be that Marlowe has it right, that the only thing to do with a Faust is to damn him, that wickedness merits final retribution, and that forgiveness is merited by goodness. Human wickedness may on the contrary be manifest in retribution as distinct from the punishment that respects the one punished, and the capacity for forgiveness in those on the way to being good. In Goethe's version, the girl Faust seduced and abandoned continues to pray for him and her prayers are also those of the whole company of heaven. I am not suggesting that we know what 'forgiveness' may mean in all circumstances, and it may have both minimal and maximal forms. It may be possible at least to be clear that we can identify moments when it may be prematurely or inappropriately requested, but that it is in words and actions of celebration and lament that we may be able to find out what it means, and that liturgy provides a context for those words and actions, hopefully without deception and delusion.

4

So to quote that much misunderstood bishop J. A. T. Robinson, 'Clothing the action with the right words is indeed of vital importance when we know what we want to express.'[8] It is essential to get this as right as we can, for who is going to 'set' the Kyrie Eleison, the Gloria or the Sanctus or the creeds unless that integrity is there? And though it tends to be the Magnificat that is treated as a 'political' text these days (because of its association with 'base communities' and liberation theology),

---

8 J. A. T. Robinson, *Liturgy Coming to Life* (London: Mowbray, 1960), v.

all the liturgical texts just mentioned are also deeply political, in that they insistently remind us where our loyalty is to lie, and thus put other supposed 'lords' in their places. And to take another clue from Robinson, it follows that our allegiance needs public expression, that we must recover the sense of obligation to be there at the liturgy (not reducible to the Eucharist), to recognize its necessity, as salt for food, yeast for bread. It is utterly maddening when someone does not turn up for rehearsals, for planning and policy meetings, absent from drafting and redrafting documents, from varied practices of commitment. Robinson's most chilling example is as follows: '"How often should I go?" is as if the disciples had asked that night, the night in which he was betrayed, "Need I be there?" There was one only who could think of leaving that evening, and when he went out it was night indeed.'⁹ Who expects absentees to be present actually to perform the play?

And Holy Communion – *koinonia hagion*, the making common of the holy, and sanctifying the common – is not undertaken by the ordained for the lay, but by the Church for the world. From this one cannot be 'dismissed' unless we have been present and have said (in some way), 'And here we offer and present unto thee, O Lord, ourselves, our souls and bodies', and have taken to ourselves the responsibility 'by life and doctrine to set forth thy true and lively word'. And we might take seriously that text in the Book of Common Prayer which is a summons to the negligent (of wider application than to Communion) which beseeches us 'for the Lord Jesus Christ's sake, that ye will not refuse to come thereto, being so lovingly called and bidden by God himself ... to feed on the banquet of that most heavenly food'. Being there is important, quite apart from anything else because it is by repetition that it all gradually sinks in: praise, gratitude, petition, confession, repentance, service, blessing,¹⁰ grace, glory, body, blood, water, fire, bread, wine,

---

9 Robinson, *Liturgy*, 60. See also Alan M. Suggate, 'In Search of a Eucharistic Social Ethic', in Oswald Bayer and Alan M. Suggate, eds, *Worship and Ethics: Lutherans and Anglicans in Dialogue* (Berlin: de Gruyter, 1996), 160–86.

10 See Helen Oppenheimer, 'Blessing', in Daniel W. Hardy and Peter

death and resurrection. It all takes time to learn, and I do not underestimate the difficulty either of convincing people that they must be there, or of sustaining their commitment to one another. We might, however, come to appreciate the glorious irony of 'liturgy' itself as having to do with work/people, public service in fact, in societies so bereft of what public service might mean.

I conclude with a somewhat different emphasis. Sacramental living in our time – and perhaps in all times and places – requires a certain sense of 'being in training', of *ascesis*, if appetites are not to be spoiled. Like forgiveness, *joie de vivre* needs care. Asceticism is about what we need to give up in order to be freed up to gain the life that matters, in relation to divine presence and all the things we see, hear, smell, taste and touch, make ceremonies of, decorate, make jokes about. Especially in societies that foster a standing temptation to assess who we are in terms of what we have, which seeps into the domestic from the public, and so constitutes 'home' for us, a renewed sacramentalism may require renewed asceticism, the capacity to say 'no' as a mark of maturity, with Lent as 'taster' – and I use the metaphor deliberately. It has something to do with that sense of travelling light I mentioned earlier. It can go badly wrong, as can a sense of the sacramental, but it may also prepare people for the 'banquet of that most heavenly food' whether they know it or not. The difficulties are expressed in Richard Wilbur's poem on 'Matthew VIII.28ff' in which the Gadarenes of the Gospel narrative declare themselves fond of wealth, putting their faith in prosperity, deeming charity inessential, and refusing to 'resign our trust in the high-heaped table and the full trough', preferring that Jesus 'shoved off'.[11]

A modern 'parable' about those who have learned not to be Gadarenes, we might say, is Isak Dinesen/Karen Blixen's

---

Sedgwick, eds, *The Weight of Glory* (Edinburgh: T & T Clark, 1991), 221–30.

11 Find the poem in David Impastato, ed., *Upholding Mystery: An Anthology of Contemporary Christian Poetry* (Oxford: Oxford University Press, 1997), 243–4.

brilliant short story 'Babette's Feast'.[12] Martine and Philippa are two sisters, once beautiful, now the elderly daughters of a devout man who had founded a party of believers whose members 'renounced the pleasures of this world, for the earth and all that it held to them was but a kind of illusion, and the true reality was the New Jerusalem toward which they were longing'. In their youth, both had been deeply admired by men who found them impossible to deal with, but one of the men eventually sends to their home a terrified, exhausted and bereaved refugee from the civil war of the 1870s in France. 'Babette can cook', he writes, and she becomes 'the dark Martha in the house of the two fair Marys', whose own fare, they told her, must be as plain as possible: 'it was the soup-pails and baskets for the poor that signified'. Twelve years later, Babette wins the French Lottery, for a friend had renewed her ticket every year. The sisters assume that the 10,000 francs will enable her to return home, but first she persuades them to let her cook a special meal in honour of their father's centenary year. The sisters and the other members of their devout group agree that 'on the day of our master we will cleanse our tongues of all taste and purify them of all delight or disgust of the senses, keeping and preserving them for the higher things of praise and thanksgiving'.

On the evening of the dinner, there is one additional guest, a nephew of one of the elderly women, himself one of the admirers of Martine in her youth. This distinguished man, now a general, expects to eat haddock accompanied by a glass of water, but the reality is astonishingly different. The devout were sitting down to a meal, 'well, so had people done at the wedding of Cana. And grace had chosen to manifest itself there, in the very wine, as fully as anywhere.' The general alone identifies the Amontillado in the first glass set before him, the 'lemonade', the succession of superb dishes. The experience takes him back to a memorable evening in a Paris café, whose chef was a woman, 'a person known all over Paris as the greatest culinary genius of her age'. The others by this stage had grown 'lighter

12 Isak Dinesen, *Anecdotes of Destiny* (Harmondsworth: Penguin, 1958), 23–68.

in weight and lighter of heart the more they ate and drank. They no longer needed to remind themselves of their vow. It was, they realized, when man has not only altogether forgotten but has firmly renounced all ideas of food and drink that he eats and drinks in the right spirit.' Spontaneously, the General gives a brief after-dinner speech about grace, which 'demands nothing from us but that we shall await it with confidence and acknowledge it in gratitude'. The guests' recollection of the evening is unclear, but they know that they have received 'one hour of the millennium'. When they leave in their state of reconciliation they fall into the new snow and are covered with it, 'as if they had indeed had their sins washed white as wool, and in this regained innocent attire were gambolling like little lambs'. '"Bless you, bless you, bless you", like an echo of the harmony of the spheres rang on all sides.' The sisters discover both that Babette has spent all her money on the feast, and that she is not returning to Paris. Moreover, she reveals that she was once the chef of the Café Anglais, and that she is indeed a great artist, whose only cry is 'Give me leave to do my uttermost'.

This brings me to my final point, which is to re-emphasize the third of my concerns, running like a connecting thread through what I have been saying. One of the reasons why our sense of liturgy is so poor is that we have lost the integration of sacramental and human creativity with redemption and the particular sacraments of the liturgy. We have lost the sense of what it is to be an artist, and have lost the artists themselves – not just painters and musicians, but poets and novelists (and others). Yet how can preaching be regenerated without the poets, or the formal structure of liturgy? And since preaching is a kind of performance for which people are 'costumed', so we need the skills of those who know what it is to communicate with their bodies – dancers as well as actors. So to conclude, the insight of Elizabeth Jennings on 'art as gesture and as sacrament': akin to 'the Presence under wine and bread' and marked by both largesse and restraint.[13]

---

13 See Brown and Fuller, eds, *Signs of Grace*, 131.

PART 2

Around the *Sanctorale*

Each of the following pieces focuses on the life of a particular individual found in the sanctorale, *the calendar of saints,[1] and they are presented in what follows as they appear in the unfolding of the liturgical year.*

---

1 See Ann's editorials in *Theology* – for example, those on Josephine Butler (*Theology* 786 (1995): 417–18) and Evelyn Underhill (*Theology* 794 (1997): 80–1). Ann often used this editorial space to discuss the lives of saints and it would be interesting to note the correlation of these publications with her sermons at or near the time the editorials went to press.

21

John Wycliffe (31 December)

If I simply ask, 'What about Wycliffe?' at least some of you may think that I am about to reflect on a certain television series detective of that name. But no, I'm concerned this morning with a John Wycliffe who died on 31 December 1384, one of those listed in our calendar for commemoration and, like some others whose death fell in the depths of winter, likely to be overlooked. This is so despite the fact that in his day he was a most controversial figure, and that in our day he should be remembered and recalled especially for the role he played in making the Scriptures available to be heard and read in the vernacular – which is what we nowadays expect.

So let us begin by reminding ourselves of what is commonly known about Wycliffe himself. He was born about 1324 near the village of Wyclif in Yorkshire, and received enough education to be recognized as someone who should go to university – to the relatively new Oxford as it happened, where he became associated with a number of its institutions, notably becoming Master of Balliol College in 1361 after a long period of study which had begun with the arts and had grown into theology. He became an ordained priest, and like others was appointed to livings well enough financed for him to be able to pay less fortunate clergy to do the work of those livings, while the financial surplus enabled him to fund his own studies in Oxford. I'm referring of course to the problem of unbeneficed clergy, clearly an abuse and one not finally disentangled until the twentieth century – not that this was one of the abuses that Wycliffe himself seems explicitly to have tackled. He may well have thought that it was too big a problem to be tackled, and given the length of time it took to sort out, he was quite right.

Once qualified as a Master of Theology he was also quickly recognized as a man of many talents (and with nerves of steel) who as it so happened held views very much in line with some of the most powerful political figures of his day – John of Gaunt, for instance. For many years, as a result, he had significant protection when criticism of his views mounted and he was in real danger of even losing his life.

The political problems of the day were indeed very serious. For instance, endless war without apparent victory meant increasing reluctance to find the taxation that would fund the conflicts, not least when a Church well endowed with rich institutions and certain wealthy clergy were exempt from taxation. Why not remove such exemption and lay hands on the endowments? And war apart, questions were rightly being raised about how the possession of great wealth was supposed to be compatible with living a Christ-like life. And why were some churchmen holding major offices of state? Did all this reflect the life of the Christian community to be found in the Acts of the Apostles, for instance?

Furthermore, as a King's chaplain, he became known as someone implacably opposed to papal supremacy in ecclesiastical affairs, not least the old problem of appointments of bishops in particular, who were important because of the roles they played in political life. And the papacy came to be in a simply ridiculous state since on the death of one pope in 1378 there were two of them until 1418 – one in Avignon and one in Rome, each with his own court. No good reason to help fund either of them? This mess provided a golden opportunity to repeat what others in Europe had said – the need to distinguish between civil and ecclesiastical power, and not to suppose that civil power was delegated by Christ to the papacy and thence to rulers. Even when that was agreed, if it ever would be, there was another problem, which was that nothing in the Gospels supported the notion that there was a great store of merit held by Christ and the saints upon which a pope could draw, so that the pope was supposed to have power to remit sin in this life and the next. Could any of this be supported from Scripture? And Wycliffe was to go further: since God alone knew who were among the elect, that group might or might not include priests like himself – the laity and the clergy were on the same footing here. This was a view hardly likely to endear him to his fellow clergy. Obviously, Wycliffe was radically re-evaluating what it was to be a priest, his own identity. And since he argued for clerical marriage, this would be another reason why over time he fell out with most of the religious orders of his day. This was important because they had a grip on the teaching of theology in the University, and he believed that they were teaching falsehoods. The crunch issue came over the meaning of what was going on in the Eucharist.

The difficulty here was that there were two views about how it was to be regarded. One venerable view was that believers were united with Christ by faith: Christ risen, ascended, glorified – especially important when the laity attended the Eucharist but did not 'receive' the sacrament except very infrequently. The other view, which crept into prominence in the second millennium, was that by the words of institution uttered by the priest (another issue about clerical power) the bread and wine became 'transubstantiated', became a different reality, Christ's body and blood, despite continuing to appear as bread and wine. Again, did the biblical accounts of the Eucharist warrant any such conviction?

The laity were of course almost wholly dependent on what their preachers told them about the meaning of whatever rites there were, for a preacher had to translate and explain the text of relevant Scriptures about the Eucharist and anything else. Would a Dominican, a Franciscan, an Augustinian and a diocesan priest necessarily give the same translation and explanation?

And that Scripture was in Latin, a translation made by Jerome and others around the turn of the fourth century – a translation that had become the Scripture of the Western Church. In Wycliffe's day, there were few indeed returning to the original languages in which the texts had been transmitted. That Latin translation had over the centuries become enmeshed with the traditions and doctrines of the Church as they had developed, and with ecclesiastical law. What people heard had to be learned by heart, so if what was taught them was mistaken or false, the matter was very serious. So if Wycliffe and others wanted reform, as indeed they did, and believing that monarch and civil authorities could achieve such reform in the Church, something had to be done about access to the text of Scripture in the vernacular, as a standard against which mistakes and falsehood and abuses could be checked. Jerome himself was a most useful predecessor in making Scripture accessible in the dominant 'professional' language of his day! Wycliffe thought that it was crucial to read Scripture in the light of the work of a great interpreter, such as Augustine. It was not a case of everyone for themselves, as it were, but at the end of the day it was crucial to obey one's conscience if at odds with authority – crucial, and always difficult in a head-on collision, however much one's conscience seemed to have been informed by scriptural texts. This issue of conscience remains absolutely central to personal integrity, depending on context, as well we know. Wycliffe was challenging claims about the exclusive teaching office of the clergy. Beyond that, his critics were surely right to ask whether there could be reform in the Church without reform in civil society, and to ask questions about the management of the dangers of possible disruption all round, given the ways in which Church and civil orders were so entwined.

Wycliffe left at least 294 sermons in English and another 224 in Latin, plus expositions of key biblical texts – the Lord's Prayer, for instance, and about 1,000 printed pages on the value and authority of Scripture. Worn out and ill, he retreated eventually to one of his livings where he died at the end of December 1384. He was fortunate to be able to die in his bed, unlike some others engaged in reform – Jan Hus and William Tyndale, for example. In 1413 a Church council ordered his books to be burned and what was left of him to be dug up and burned and cast into the nearest river – a strange fate for the remains of an Oxford academic priest who became such a catalyst for change, a 'one-off' never matched in later centuries.

We have no precise knowledge of how much of what became the Bible in English came from him and how much from others, which does not much matter since most translation was a cooperative effort. What matters is that he was an instigator of a movement that exited from Oxford and lasted for another century at what we might call grass-roots level, and survived serious persecution by the authorities. Wycliffe never intended to start off such a movement, but those who had taken in what he said fed into the strengths of reform, aided by the advent of printed books and the availability of Scripture in the vernacular – the first complete English Bible and the first Scots dialect Bible both appeared in the first quarter of the sixteenth century. Burning Wycliffe's bones did nothing to stifle the debates to which he contributed so vigorously, and to him and to others, we owe a very great debt.

22

Thomas Aquinas (28 January)

We are invited by readings and hymns at this point in the Christian year to think about 'vocation'. So as it is the beginning of the university semester, and as it happens this coming week includes the commemoration of St Thomas Aquinas as 'Teacher of the Faith', let us focus on Thomas, surely one of the greatest contributors to any university's consideration of theology in any century. Not that I think even his biblical commentaries are given a great deal of attention in the Divinity School just at present, as once they may have been, pre the Reformation. Just one preliminary point about why 28 January is his day of commemoration when he died on 7 March in 1274, for often, but not always, a day of commemoration is that person's death day. Thomas is too important to be overlooked in Lent, as he might be if remembered in March every year – so 28 January was chosen because it is the date of the translation of his relics to the church of his order in Toulouse.

In St Andrews we have no relics of St Thomas directly, but we do still have the remnants of the Dominican Priory on South Street, and once upon a time members of the Order of Preachers – their proper title – would have been seen around the place in their white cassocks and black overgarment and cloak. They were a comparatively young order, mendicants, beggars, like the Franciscans, but founded by Dominic from Castile out of a concern for the growth of heresy, and its consequences both for Church and good order in society. Hence, of course, Dominicans – and the pun on Dominic's name, *Dominicanes*: God's dogs, the dogs of God, and perhaps by implication hunting dogs, heresy hunters. So bearing in mind the pun and the colours of their habits, you may sometimes see in paintings in Italy the inclusion of some lively-looking black and white animals – they stand in for Dominicans.

Dominic died in 1221. His life and character never captured the European imagination as did that of St Francis, but he was amazingly successful in the development of his new order, founded in 1216 – all of them to be priests, with a network of priories stretching from Hungary to his own Spain and northward to Denmark and Sweden. They were forbidden the settled, stable life of the Benedictine abbeys, and were to be as footloose as the Franciscans, begging their way wherever they were required to preach. Begging had hitherto been forbidden to the clergy, so that was a major reason why they were regarded as troublesome by established and authoritative persons like bishops. Interestingly, they were forbidden to ride on horseback – and considering the young men of aristocratic family they attracted, this would be one mark of their new social status, as was the prohibition on riding in vehicles drawn by animals. They had to walk everywhere, meaning everywhere – from Naples to Paris to Viterbo to Perugia to Cologne to Rome to Toulouse to Lyons – and it may have led to some interesting problems – begging for shoe and boot leather as well as for food. When one of Thomas' fellow Dominicans became Bishop of Regensburg he continued to tramp around his diocese, quickly earning himself the nickname of 'The Boot' or 'The Clog'.

But how did Thomas come to join this company of intellectual beggars who persistently headed for the towns, preferably where there was already a 'university' – that word originally meaning the whole company of teachers and taught, and then also the totality of what was likely to be taught there – subject areas such as theology, philosophy, law and medicine. Thomas was born in 1224 or 1225, just a few years after the death of Dominic and a year or so before the death of Francis. He was the youngest of seven (with the family name of Aquino), fortunate in having a couple of sisters who seemed to appreciate the baby in the family more than did his brothers. The family was well connected to the region's aristocracy, and it would have been perfectly reasonable to suppose that this youngest son would follow his brothers into military service. So he would have been taught to ride at a very early age, and it would have been hoped that he would learn the martial arts of the day in due course. It was not unknown, however, for a youngest son to consider a monastic vocation, and the five-year-old Thomas was sent to begin his scholastic education in the nearby abbey of Monte Cassino, where his uncle was abbot. He might quite possibly have ended up as abbot himself one day, given the family from which he emerged. It must have been the monks there who realized that they had an exceptionally clever child on their hands, and it may have been at Monte Cassino that the growing boy heard about the new Order of Preachers, one of the two major new groups of 'beggars' in the Church. In any event, by the time he was 15, he had exasperated and embarrassed his family beyond endurance by making it clear that the Order of Preachers was his choice. It may also be that during this time of growing up Thomas learned to keep his mouth shut when with his family – no good arguing with people who simply would not listen to him. So he grew into a big man who kept his thoughts to himself, and his nickname in the Dominicans was the Dumb Ox. He might not have made it into the Order. Learning of his family's determination to prevent him joining, the abbot of Monte Cassino attempted to get Thomas out of the way by sending him to Paris or to the smart and brand new university of Naples, but his brothers waylaid the little party. They kidnapped Thomas, imprisoning him for at least a year in one of the family's castles. It seems possible that it was one of his sisters who got him out and he made good his escape, moving around as the Dominicans thought best, and with a crucial period of study in Cologne, where in 1248 the foundation stone of the cathedral had been laid.

Eventually, at the age of 27, Thomas was sent to Paris, where the Order had been dug in since 1217, and as a group not altogether welcome – there were times when their hostel was under armed guard! For one thing, if people went to hear the friars preach, such cash as might go into their collecting plate didn't go to the parish church. Once fully qualified, Thomas from the Order of Preachers and Bonaventura from the Franciscans were two obvious appointees to chairs in Theology, according to the university chancellor, deputed by the pope to make such appointments. Bonaventura escaped the controversy because he was called away to be head of the Franciscans, so Thomas had to bear the brunt of the row. Blocking someone else's promotion? Taking their jobs? Did beggars take a salary? There were boycotted classes, lectures interrupted, being refused recognition by other professors, even when there was only one from each Order. Occasionally there were unexpected complications when an existing professor decided to join the Order of Preachers, which really put the cat among the pigeons!

Thomas, fortunately, was a master of the capacity to get on with things no matter what. Since he never wasted time talking, he was always working things out in his head, ready to write at the first opportunity. But he did talk, of course – as a brilliant teacher. For instance, he ran open disputations, a couple a week between 1256 and 1259. There are records of about 500 of these, in which he trained the arts graduates attending how to listen most carefully to those with whom they disagreed; to be able to restate their opponent's arguments better than their opponent had in the first place; and, however heated the argument, to exemplify respect, courtesy, even gratitude for the presence of one another. The pursuit of truth was the primary goal.

Thomas was never allowed to stay very long in any one place, being called upon for one reason or another from the papal court to the next city or priory, but he made good use of all that walking time – working things out in his head, and either writing up his material himself or, when provided with a companion and secretary, Reginald of Piperno, dictating his material. He was also able to manage the work of a group of secretaries if given the opportunity. So to take just one of his massive contributions to the clarification of the whole tradition of Christian theology, his Summary contains 38 treatises, 612 questions subdivided into 3,120 articles, with about 10,000 criticisms or objections to the topic under discussion proposed and answered. It's a sort of skeleton record of how discussions were conducted in his seminars. He is kept alive for us at least minimally, even if we do not study his theology, by some great hymns for the Feast of Corpus Christi, if you could look those up and bear Thomas in mind – we will meet him again later in the year.

To conclude: Thomas' life in many ways from childhood on was stacked with controversy, much of it to do with the use he made of the rediscovered works of the great philosopher Aristotle, so helpfully mediated to the Latin West by the philosophers and theologians and brilliant translators of Islam. But at the core, he knew exactly what he was after for everyone to whom he preached:

> Three kinds of knowledge are necessary to man for his salvation: the knowledge of what he must believe, the knowledge of that for which he must pray, and the knowledge of what he must do. The first is taught in the creeds of our Faith, the second in the prayer of the Lord, the third in the commandments.[1]

And when he died at the abbey of Fossanova in 1274 they did not sing the Mass for the Dead for him but the Mass for a Holy Confessor, which begins, 'The mouth of the just man shall meditate wisdom and his tongue shall speak judgment: the law of his God is in his heart.' And at his canonization in 1323 he was remembered as 'soft-spoken, easy in conversation, cheerful and bland of countenance, good in soul, generous in conduct, most patient, most prudent, all radiant with charity and gentle piety, and wondrously compassionate to the poor'. An 'angelic Doctor' indeed!

So let us keep Thomas in mind when we find people who have an intellectual vocation to serve God – even if not as 'beggars'. It's far from clear that our churches today (with rare exceptions) do in fact honour such vocations. It seems to me that we have a lot to learn from Thomas.

---

1 George G. Leckie, ed., *Thomas Aquinas, Concerning Being and Essence* (New York: Appleton Company, 1937), 27.

23

Scholastica (10 February)

We are invited to commemorate St Scholastica on 10 February – a saint in both Western and Eastern church traditions. 'St Who?' you might well ask! Some information and reminders then.

Let us begin by thinking why someone might be called 'Scholastica' and what her name might mean. Think of words that are perfectly familiar – school, schooling, *schola cantorum* (a choir). These all have to do with groups of people brought together for a particular purpose. What of individuals? The obvious one is *scholasticus* – a learned man. So, perhaps, a new coinage – *scholastica*, a learned woman, a rare phenomenon in many times and places. So St Scholastica, twin sister of the Benedict who founded the great lay order of Benedictines. As lay, that meant one hurdle fewer for women who wanted to join, because one of the attractions of the Benedictine life was the chance of what we would now call higher education. There are many worse fates than retreat to a book-lined cell! Some might achieve this at home, to begin with, but the time might well come when staying at home was no longer an option. Maybe Scholastica was a family name for a very clever daughter, or maybe it was a name she took on joining the order her brother was establishing.

But why early monasticism anyway? The point is that in Christianity you have a choice. On the one hand, there is the option of lineage, blood relationships, a network of kin, children and a future for them through the generations (and in many times and places that could be at a very high cost to women in pregnancy and childbirth). On the other hand, there is the perspective gained by belief in and hope for the resurrection, and the gospel promise that in the life to come there will be no marriage or giving in marriage because resurrection has to do with the denial of death. So there remains marriage and lineage and a future of a kind despite death, or a different kind of life: celibacy, in anticipation of the resurrection. This did not mean a solitary life in contrast to the life one might live in a network of family and kin. Celibacy was to be lived in community. To be a 'monk' is to become capable in principle of living on one's own, but few may be capable of doing so without long training in community – hence religious orders of various kinds.

Benedict himself seems to have left home as what we now call a teenager, while his sister remained there, and from what we know of their later relationship this may have meant misery for her after he left. An effort at education in Rome was enough to send Benedict into near solitude in remote caves, where, after about three years, groups of men began to associate themselves with him, ten or twelve in each with a leader, establishing themselves in caves nearby. Eventually he established what became a great abbey on Mount Cassino. Gradually, over a period of time, he put together the famous Benedictine Rule for his lay community, a Rule notable for its balance and moderation as Benedict reflected on previous attempts, from which he could select what seemed best.

And at this point, we need to go back behind *schola* to the meaning of its Greek antecedent, *skolé*, meaning a 'pause', a 'break', a moment of 'leisure' in the sense of taking time for thought, for reflection, and practising that as a strength, a virtue – taking time for reflection very seriously. What might this have to do with monastic life? The key text is Psalm 46.10: 'Be still, and know that I am God' – with the verb form of *skolé*. Take time for God, we might say. Hence in the Benedictine monastery all the work that had to be done was punctuated by the Opus Dei, the work of God – the times of prayer and praise organized so that the whole psalter was chanted through once a week. So every week the monks came across 'Be still, and know that I am God' – as if they needed reminding!

So what of Benedict's much-loved sister? At some point in her life, most probably after the death of her father, she came under the care of her brother, and some five miles from his life on Mount Cassino, she, as Scholastica, was to be found in a small community of sisters. She was the learned lady and, like the men in the nearby monastery, committed to stability – no gallivanting about; conversion of manners/morals; and obedience to the abbot. This group of women would also have to sustain the Opus Dei, the life of adoration of God.

We know a little about Scholastica through the writings of Pope Gregory the Great, himself a former monk and abbot who thoroughly understood what Benedict had achieved and the hazards he had to negotiate. Benedict and Scholastica met once a year, with Benedict and a few companions visiting her in her community. Gregory gives us what I think is a humorous account in his glimpse of the kind of relationship between the twins, aged 63, in 543. Towards the end of the day, Scholastica pleaded with her brother not to leave, so that they could continue to talk about 'the joys of the heavenly life'. Benedict, quite properly, was anxious to get back to the monastery, as he and his companions were required to be there overnight. 'Now the sky was clear and cloudless'. Scholastica folded her hands, placed them on the table, and bowed her head in prayer to God. When she lifted her head, a storm broke out – torrential rain, thunder and lightning, making it impossible for Benedict to leave. Her abbot had no doubt that she was responsible. 'May Almighty God forgive thee, my sister. What is this thing that thou has done?' She replied in all too familiar words: 'I asked thee, and thou wouldst not listen to me. I asked my Lord, and he has heard me. Go now if thou canst …' Benedict had to remain against his will, until the storm finished and light returned. 'And they spent the night in vigil and comforted each other with holy converse of spiritual things.'

Benedict was soon to realize why Scholastica had wanted him to stay, because within three days she had died. He sent some of his monks to bring her body to the monastery and placed it in the grave that he had prepared for them both. When Benedict came to die he was carried to his oratory to pray, and died there. 'So it happened to these two, whose minds had ever been united in the Lord, that even in the grave their bodies were not separated.' It is unfortunately not possible to visit them there, since their bodies became the targets of relic hunters, so neither was allowed to remain in the spot Benedict had chosen – another and different story.

So there is something about St Scholastica: the love of learning and the desire for God, freedom in celibacy from so much of what might otherwise have been expected of her; and whatever we make of all that, we share something of her commitment to the life-long adoration of God. 'Be still, and know that I am God', in the words of the psalmist. Take time for God – else why would we all be here this morning, or on other occasions?

24

Catherine of Siena (29 April)

Yesterday, 29 April, happens to mark the anniversary of the death at the age of 33 of Catherine of Siena, in Rome in 1380.[1] And for that day we find her listed in the Church of England's *Alternative Service Book* under the heading of Lesser Festival Commemorations as a mystic – a designation she shares in the ASB with Julian of Norwich and Teresa of Avila. In the Roman Catholic tradition she also shares with the latter the dignity of having in 1970 been accorded the title of Doctor of the Church. I note in passing that no women in the Church of England's list are yet deemed to have been Teachers of the Faith!

By comparison with Teresa, Anglicans seem to have neglected Catherine and what she may represent for us – with the notable exception of that remarkable nineteenth-century reformer Josephine Butler, whose own day of commemoration falls on 30 May. With these preliminary points in mind, therefore, I would like to take the opportunity provided by this occasion to make a small contribution to the consideration of Catherine.

Catherine's book, her *Dialogue*, a biography and other memoirs of her were among the earliest books in print, her *Dialogue* indeed in an English version by 1519. The book, the biography and the memoirs, copies of her letters and prayers – all would be needed by those who wanted to advance her claim to sanctity, declared as it happened some 80 years after her death. And all these writings are now available to us in new translations and editions to provoke us to ask in our time what we might now make of her.

---

1 Note that the Church of England at last deemed some women to be 'Teachers of the Faith' with the Common Worship books from 2000.

She is supposed to have been born on 25 March, the Feast of the Annunciation, in 1347, just before one of the grim years of the Black Death. She had a twin sister who died when the babies were only a few days old. One more daughter was to be born, named Giovanna after the twin who had died, but she herself was to die when Catherine was about 16. So Catherine was almost the youngest in a family of 25. To a brother at odds with their mother later in life she was to write:

> You forget her labour in bringing you into the world, the milk with which she fed you, and all the trouble she had in rearing you and the others. You may want to say that she didn't look after us, but I say that isn't true. Her great care and concern for you and your brother have cost her dearly. And even if it were true, *you* are still the one who is under an obligation to her, not she to you. She did not get her flesh from you, but gave you hers.

Of the children running round her mother's kitchen she was to say, 'If decency allowed it, I would never stop kissing them', but she knew the hazards of losing them, of bereavement, and of her own possible death – a much-loved sister died in childbirth – and such eventualities might have helped to prompt her, as it did other young women, to think she would prefer marriage to Christ. And there were those inside as well as outside her family to encourage her.

There was a Dominican church in Siena, and the Friars Preachers there included a young man, Tommaso della Fonte, who had been brought up in her own family after being orphaned by an outbreak of the plague. It was Tommaso who encouraged her to cut off her hair, one of the ways she could show her family her determined resistance to their plans for her. She could surely only have got away with it because she was utterly secure in their love, not least that of her father, who allowed her a form of seclusion in their home for about three years. Of course Christ would later address her as 'My daughter Catherine', 'O daughter whom I so love', 'O dearest gentlest daughter'!

This daughter was being transformed from the family's darling into a different and rather unexpected person, unnerving to herself as to them, and to her Dominican protectors and confessors. These in particular were crucial to her future role, for without them what she undertook would have been simply impossible for a mere laywoman, unmarried or not. We might compare the fate of Margery Kempe in fifteenth-century England. So that period of seclusion depended not only on the goodwill of her father and family, but on that of the Dominicans. They found themselves confronted with a determinedly unmarriageable and perhaps almost unmanageable 16-year-old, clever, imaginative, passionate and deeply ascetic, who wanted her way with them too. Not for her what was then on offer as the Dominican vocation for women.

Dominic himself, we may recall, had been willing to provide a house of his Order for women retrieved from the Cathar heresy, and the Dominicans had negotiated their way through all the unpredictable as well as predictable problems experienced by the old and the newer orders either attempting or refusing to cope with the religious aspirations of women. It was to the credit of the fifth Master General of the Order of Friars Preachers, Humbert, author of a significant text, *On the Formation of Preachers*, who recognized the obligations of the Order to women. However, these mendicants committed themselves to the support of houses for women who were to be enclosed contemplatives.

The Order had claimed for themselves both preaching and the licensing of preachers (rather than leaving all this to bishops alone) under the rubric, as it were, of Paul's text in second Corinthians: 'We preach not ourselves but Jesus Christ our Lord.' They had moved into the major cities where they could tackle the intellectual battles of their day as they begged for their subsistence. It was as yet inconceivable, unfortunately, that there could be priories where women too would study, so that they also might teach (if not actually preach), hear confession and counsel penitents. But it looks as though this is just the sort of vocation Catherine was looking for – so she managed the next best thing. She won for herself association with those women, usually widows, who wore the black and white habit of the Sisters of Penance of St Dominic, lived in their own homes and served the needs of the sick and poor. These women were understandably cautious about taking on one so young, but were persuaded; and Catherine's period of seclusion before she rejoined her family and neighbours was a very important time of preparation for what she presumably thought would be the kind of life these Sisters led. She learned to read – most likely texts with which she was already familiar from having heard them, such as the liturgy and the New Testament, all later to be transposed, as we find them in her own writings, into her own Sienese vernacular. And she learned from the Friars. She was beginning to get her intellectual framework together. For instance, as she was later to put it, God says to her (among many other things), 'Open your mind's eye and look within me, and you will see the dignity and beauty of my reasoning creature.' Even more movingly, perhaps, her emendation of Luke 1.38: 'I will tell you something. When God created man, he said to him: "Be it done according to your will", that is, "I make you free, subject only to myself."' Or again, she tells someone that Christ 'has clothed us in the strongest of all clothing: in the garment of love, fastened with the clasp of free will (so that you do it up and undo it as you choose). If a man wants to throw off this garment of charity, he can; and if he wants to keep it on, he can do that too.'

What she was also doing was learning what were for her the difficult virtues of courage and patience – virtues she would need in order to care for the afflicted, and for the other tasks she was quite unable to foresee. Above all, she practised the penances that would bring about the dispossession of self that would free her for others. So she asks Christ, 'My Lord, where were you when my heart was disturbed by all those temptations?' He replies, 'I was in your heart.' She's not satisfied. 'May your truth always be preserved, Lord, and all reverence to your Majesty ... but how can I possibly believe that you were in my heart when it was full of ugly filthy thoughts?' He helps her to work it out. 'Did those thoughts and temptations bring content or sorrow, delight or displeasure to your heart?'

She replies, 'The greatest sorrow and displeasure.' 'Well then', says the Lord, 'Who was hidden at the centre of your heart?'

Inevitably the serious practice of her religion – intellectual, affective, practical as it was – transformed her. Already pushing at all sorts of boundaries, she became an increasingly controversial figure. While she succoured the poor and the sick, nursed and buried victims of the plague, she began to collect around herself her own 'family'. There were two widows, among the first to act as her secretaries, Franciscans as well as Dominicans, the occasional poet and painter; and that all too English-seeming near recluse, William Flete, Augustinian friar and Bachelor of Cambridge University. She had an astonishing capacity to secure the protection and the resources she needed, not least for when she began to travel.

A particularly significant visit must have been the first major trip, which was to Florence, to a Chapter of the Friars Preachers in May 1374. Raymond of Capua may already have known her in Siena, but from about this time, and once convinced of her authority, this future Master General of his Order became first her confessor and later her biographer.

What, briefly, may we attend to in the latter part of her life? It coincides with the disastrous conflict between Florence and the Holy See, the papacy in Avignon, political misrule, and pitiless slaughter in the city states of Italy. Hence her attempts to influence the course of events by letter writing, and her travels between Florence, Pisa, Avignon and Rome. It is in this context that she would insist, 'You know that peace is given with the mouth' – to mercenaries, to brutal churchmen, to corrupt governors. The last decade of her life corresponds with the period when Wycliffe entered royal service, and came to the attention of Gregory XI. We might be hard put to it to decide between the relative merits of Wycliffe's and Catherine's rhetoric of denunciation. To that same pope (*'dolcissimo babbo mio'* – roughly, 'sweetest daddy mine') she writes in effect that his government stinks.

She tried to divert combatants and mercenaries into another crusade. Medieval maps after all showed Jerusalem at the heart of the world, lying in the possession of Islam. We may well find that difficult without disputing her desire for peace. She wanted to reconcile clergy and laity; she hoped for some form of conciliar government in the Church. She learned at last to write, at the age of 30; and, above all, she dictated, wrote and revised her book, her *Dialogue*. In her opening words:

> A soul rises up, restless with tremendous desire for God's honour and the salvation of souls. She has for some time exercised herself in virtue and has become accustomed to dwelling in the cell of self-knowledge in order to know better God's goodness toward her since upon knowledge follows love. And loving, she seeks to pursue truth and clothe herself in it.
>
> But there is no way she can so savour and be enlightened by this truth as in continual humble prayer, grounded in the knowledge of herself and of God. For by such prayer the soul is united with God, following in the footsteps of Christ crucified, and through desire and affection and the union of love he makes of her another himself.

In the *Dialogue*, as in her letters, we find her theological reason for whatever she claims to be necessary for the form of the Church of her day, and the exercise of its authority. It is because the Church holds the 'keys of the blood' – mediates to humanity God's unimaginably generous means of redemption. And for me her utter conviction about the truth of this is revealed in all its appalling clarity in one of her letters, written to Raymond of Capua, when she is in her late twenties. It's one of the very rare letters in which she describes her own actions.

You might expect to find somewhere in her work what we read in an earlier letter to friars preaching in Lent (either 1372 or 1373): that God's Son 'rushed to give himself to the shame of the cross, and to associate with malefactors, public sinners, and outcasts of all kinds'. She adds that 'you cannot set a law or limit on charity: it is oblivious of self and quite un-self seeking'. Even so, the later letter is astonishing in all its horror. For Christ's making of Catherine 'another himself', as she somewhat dangerously put it, a Christ who committed himself to outcasts, becomes transparent in connection with the execution of Niccol di Toldo, a young Perugian condemned to death in Siena for speaking disrespectfully of the Sienese government. By her own account, she not only saw him through making his last confession and his last mass but, finding him terrified, she said to him, 'Courage, dearest brother. We shall soon be at the wedding. *You* will be going to it bathed in the sweet blood of God's Son and with the sweet name of Jesus on your lips. Don't let it slip from your mind for an instant. I shall be waiting for you at the place of execution', as indeed she was.

And she says, 'He laid himself down with great meekness; then I stretched out his neck and bent over him, speaking to him of the blood of the Lamb. His lips murmured only "Jesus" and "Catherine", and he was still murmuring when I received his head into my hands, while my eyes were fixed on the divine Goodness as I said, "*I will.*"' She saw Christ receive him, the hands of the Holy Spirit sealing him into Christ's open side. And she wrote, 'He did such a lovely thing – one last gesture that would melt a thousand hearts (and no wonder, seeing that he was already experiencing the divine sweetness). He looked back, like a bride who pauses on the bridegroom's threshold to look back and bow her thanks to her escort.' Catherine, left behind, envied him.

I am completely incompetent to comment on Catherine's experience of God or Christ but I find this particular incident almost overwhelming in its charity, its neighbour-love, in her capacity to commit herself to someone undergoing public execution. It is here above all, for me at least, that she proclaims Christ as her Lord, and shows herself to have been one of his servants.

25

Josephine Butler (30 May)

My address is I believe suitable for Ascensiontide, since I am concerned today with the remembrance of someone we may believe is presently to be found in the company of the risen and ascended Christ. The person I wish to bring to mind is Josephine Butler, now commemorated on the day of her baptism, 30 May 1828, and who grew up to put herself alongside women who were on the edge of destitution and social ruin.

Josephine was born not a Butler but a Grey, one of the Northumbrian network that included the Grey who was key to passing not only the 1832 Reform Bill but the 1824 Bill that abolished slavery in British colonies. Josephine's father, John, and her mother, Hannah, were both deeply committed Christians, alike representing to Josephine and her brothers and sisters, 'purity of heart … innocency of life … constancy in love'. And her father was wholly free of what Josephine called 'a peculiarity of modern, as of ancient barbarism, i.e. the undervaluing of the female sex'. Josephine's family offered her a great deal – much freedom in their life on the estates in Northumberland of which her father was manager; an international perspective gained from the visitors who came to consult him; good education for the girls; self-confidence and courage gained in part by riding the estates with her father and hunting with her brothers; and above all, well thought-out convictions. Not for nothing was the adult Josephine to be associated in certain contexts with the saying that 'principles know not the name of mercy'.

It was as a Grey in her family home that she learned about justice, and gained the stamina and determination to withstand commonly held opinion. And as she and others had learned from the campaigns to abolish both slave-holding and slave-trading, it was apparent that immovable social arrangements could be made to change. It was, however, as a Butler that she found the courage to act in public in a way almost unprecedented for a woman of her social class and at a time when women might doubt their competence even to take the minutes of a committee meeting, and when for them to sign a petition might seem an act of extraordinary self-assertion.

Josephine's husband, George, came from a family in which the men became headmasters of public schools, deans of cathedrals, and masters of university colleges. In marrying George, Josephine found herself with some very distinguished brothers-in-law, and in her husband, a man who gave her unequivocal support. They first met when George visited Northumberland from his post as tutor at University College, Durham between 1848 and 1850, and they were married in 1852. They went to Oxford when George was appointed to a post there, and it was in her own drawing room in her first home in Oxford that Josephine first learned how humiliating it could be to be female. A discussion of Mrs Gaskell's novel *Ruth* revealed to her that some of her male guests believed that a moral lapse in a woman was immensely worse than in a man, though no justification for such a belief was ever produced. It seemed also to be believed that a 'pure' woman must remain absolutely ignorant of some evils in the world, albeit, as Josephine was to write, 'they bore with murderous cruelty on other women'.

Far from shunning women supposedly 'guilty' of 'moral lapses', Josephine went out of her way to help them, despite being advised by a very senior cleric of Oxford University to maintain silence and take no further action. For instance, she came to know of one young woman, seduced by an academic and abandoned by him, who was serving out a sentence in Newgate prison for infanticide. On her release, she joined the Butler household as a servant, the first of many women given such shelter and employment with them. It was George himself who prevented her from becoming 'a solitary, wounded, and revolted heart', which would certainly have limited her usefulness. Justice to women was never a matter about which he needed convincing, though neither of them could have foreseen just where this might take Josephine.

When George became vice-principal of Cheltenham College, Josephine was rescued from a society where she could not always be comfortable and in Cheltenham they at first found renewed happiness, with the birth of their third son, and then their one and only daughter, Eva. The death of six-year-old Eva in a tragic fall in 1864 (running to meet her parents on their return home, and falling from a balustrade to land almost at their feet) had a most profound effect on Josephine in particular. Death in childhood was far from uncommon, as well everyone knew from bitter first-hand experience. Not everyone, however, was driven by a crisis of faith such a loss might provoke not only to a deeper trust in God but also to a passionate concern for the lives of those children who did survive, irrespective of whether they were of one's own family group. Children were far too precious to be subject to violence and abuse if Josephine could prevent it.

George's move in 1866 to become principal of a school in Liverpool fortunately took them away from the home where they were constantly reminded of Eva's death, and Josephine then threw herself into some of the causes that were expected of someone in her position. Thus she became president of the North of England Council for the Higher Education of Women, in an age when it was claimed that education for women would make them 'unwomanly' (whatever that might mean) and 'hard, unlovely, pedantic, and disinclined for domestic duties'. It seems rarely if at all observed that this was also an indictment of the education on offer to men. Josephine knew perfectly well how important education was if women were to live beyond subsistence level, for in her day governesses and teachers were sometimes literally starving. For by 1861, as she had discovered, there were already two and a half million women working for their own subsistence, 43,000 of them as labourers. As Josephine remarked, this was 'a fact worthy of remembrance when it is said that women are too weak to serve in haberdashers' shops'.

Beyond the campaign for women's education, Liverpool provided endless scope for charitable activity as a city in which thousands of the population lived crammed into cellars. Thereupon Josephine worked for the destitute and the dying, and for women imprisoned. She also began to appeal to women of her own class to claim their respect not only for themselves but for the very poorest of women. For she found in some women's lives at least one analogue of slavery, and that was the sheer intimidation of women by violence. As she said: 'If we compare the slight penalties inflicted for cruelties practised on women and children with those imposed for injury or property or the wounding of a stag, the property of a Duke, we cannot wonder at the low estimate, in England, of the worth of women.' Then as now, women had by far the greater chance of being on the receiving end of violence in their own homes and elsewhere than had men, and considerably greater difficulty in finding justice for their suffering.

Here then was a beautiful woman married to an ordained minister of the established Church, with an unquestionable social position expressed in everything she wore and everything she wrote and spoke, deeply involved in some of the causes of her day. It all seems admirable, and so it was. But it was in connection with one great cause that she found her particular vocation, and for this especially she is commemorated. For Josephine became committed not just to the 'respectable poor' but to the women who had become outcasts of society, who lived in a kind of social hell, and who needed what seemed to her a Christ-like liberation from their miseries. Of course she could support and set up refuges for prostitutes, one of the well-tried ways of aiding some of the women who had probably been tipped into prostitution out of the sheer necessity of finding roof, food and clothing, not least for their dependent children. Not for nothing does Proverbs 6.26 observe that a prostitute may be had for a loaf of bread – somewhat analogous to owning a slave for however short a time, as Josephine perceived.

To her horror, Josephine discovered just how young some prostitutes were – 13, just a year past what was then the age of consent. Some were on the run from homes where they had been abused, and some had been seduced and abandoned. Yet others were the empty-headed daughters of families too short of resources to educate their daughters as well as their sons. And on the bodies of some of the most resistant were to be found the scars of whippings and beatings from attempts to make them 'submissive' to what was expected of them in brothels. Whatever their age, they were about to face new and legally enforced intimidation of a kind familiar on mainland Europe (first introduced in Napoleonic France) but now brought to the United Kingdom. It was in this connection that Josephine found a role that launched her on to public platforms, made her able to face parliamentary commissions as the only woman called to give evidence and deal with police officers, medical practitioners and prison warders, both at home and in main- land Europe when her campaigns extended there.

The major crisis in this stage of Josephine's life came when she had turned 40. At this time the Contagious Diseases Acts had come into being, between 1864 and 1869 – five years during which women had time to face the implications not just for prostitutes but in principle for all women. For the Acts (first in force in garrison towns and naval bases and gradually extended beyond them) made it possible for any woman merely believed by a policeman to be a prostitute (and without his having to produce a shred of evidence for his belief) to be hauled before a single Justice of the Peace. And she would stand there, without any legal representation, faced with a dis- graceful choice. If she refused medical examination for sexually transmitted disease she was sentenced to imprisonment with hard labour. If she consented to medical examination she thus incriminated herself as a prostitute, and if found to be 'diseased' she was compulsorily confined in a special hos- pital. Either way led to social ruin, especially if she had to find employment simply to survive. Her most likely form of employment on release was only too obvious. The War Office and the Admiralty might well be concerned with the health of the men at their disposal, but the Acts were directed at women, held to be uniquely responsible for the transmission of venereal disease. It was hardly surprising that women and men alike should fight against the double standard of morality endorsed by the Acts, deeming necessary the availability of women free of disease for the use of men of any occupation or class. What was astonishing was that Josephine and others should be outraged not just by the impact of the Acts on the lives of working-class women, easily identifiable by their dress and by being out and about on foot at all hours; not just by the legally sanctioned medical assaults on the innocent as well as the not so innocent; not just by the surveillance and harassment of the friendless and homeless women and girls whose lives she had seen all too much in Liverpool – but outraged by the effect of the Acts on prostitutes themselves, already among the social outcasts of their day, now with that status legally reinforced.

It took Josephine three months in 1869 to resolve to accept the invitation to become President of the Ladies National Association for the Repeal of the Contagious Diseases Acts, with Quaker, Salvationist, Dissenting and Nonconformist women focused on organizing opposition to the Acts. By her own account, Josephine fled from God for those three months, hoping that if she threw herself into her existing causes, she would not be required to do more. But then she found that the thought of this atrocity killed any sense of charity within her, and hindered her prayers. She prayed for 'a way of being angry without sin', to find a way of living with 'a deep, well-governed and lifelong hatred of all such injustice, tyranny, and cruelty', in combination with a gift of divine compassion. Could God mean *her*, a Grey, a Butler, 'to rise in revolt and rebellion'? And how was she to distinguish this appalling call to conflict from mere self-assertion? She may also have guessed and feared that for the first time in her life she might have to endure both physical intimidation and verbal abuse, as certainly she did. Could she open her mouth in public to discuss responsibility for venereal disease and the lives of prostitutes? What would be the effect on George and her sons? Would the family network support her? One quite unexpected slur was that it was because of marital unhappiness that she drove herself from home – a slur the more deeply hurtful because it was George himself who waited in patience during those three late summer months for her to think the matter through. He unhesitatingly endorsed her decision to head the campaign, or what Josephine unsurprisingly called not the 'repeal' but the 'abolition' of the Acts.

The campaign was to absorb half their married life together, and lasted beyond their last move, to Winchester, when George was appointed to a canonry there. But abolition was finally achieved in 1886, managed by skilled and sympathetic parliamentarians. This was just one year after the age of consent for girls was raised from 12 to 16, another of the campaigns in which Josephine played a crucial role in her determination to protect young girls from prostitution and to destroy the cross-Channel trade in girls. She would rightly have been horrified at the continuing phenomenon of child trafficking and prostitution in our own day, given her large-heartedness for children in particular, as well as for those women she never refused to consider as outcasts from the human community. It was at the height of the campaign to get the age of consent raised to 16 waged in tandem with the leaders of the newly formed Society for the Prevention of Cruelty to Children that she was seen and remembered by Henry Scott Holland, then a canon of St Paul's, later a regius professor in Oxford. He knew that what drove Josephine on was her grief for Eva, transformed into a determination to protect girls from abuse. Hence it was appropriate to sing Scott Holland's 'Judge Eternal, throned in splendour' at the beginning of this morning's service, remembering Josephine Butler and how she came in her own person to embody resistance to the marginalization and dehumanization of any human being, no matter what their manner of life, believing them most truly to be embraced by Christ in his humanity, as she was herself.

26

Mary of Magdala (22 July)

Let us remind ourselves of one of the most important and fascinating saints not just within the Christian tradition but in our wider culture. For instance, recall 'I don't know how to love him' from Tim Rice's *Jesus Christ, Superstar* or Michelle Roberts' *The Wild Girl* or Dan Brown and *The Da Vinci Code* ... all of which I will ignore this morning as we rethink some features of the Christian tradition – within the four Gospels in particular.

To begin with, think of her context: Magdala, one of those fishing villages from which Jesus of Nazareth drew some of his disciples. What is it in her story that takes her from her home and makes her, together with Mary the mother of Jesus, one of only two women to have the creed said or sung on their feast day? She lived in territory then as now under occupation and long-standing conflict. In such times and places it could be trust in divine mercy and resurrection as a visible expression of divine vindication that sustains those faithful to God in the most appalling circumstances. Think back a century and a half to the time of the Maccabean martyrs – the family of the Maccabees having taken up arms to purify their land from the corruptions of their day – a conflict that led to the Roman occupation of Mary of Magdala's time. At the death of the men of her family – seven sons in just one day – their mother, filled with courage exhorted them (2 Maccabees 7.22–23) by proclaiming: 'I cannot tell how you came into my womb, for I neither gave you breath nor life, neither was it I that formed the members of everyone of you. But doubtless the Creator of the world, who formed the generation of man, and found out the beginning of all things, will also by his own mercy give you breath and life again, as you now regard not your own selves for his law's sake.' With that example in mind, let me suggest that from a very shaky start, Mary Magdalene turned into something like the mother of the Maccabean martyrs, for of the different 'Marys' named in the Gospels, she is the only one consistently named as being present near the Crucified One, so we might just hazard a guess that she might have been there and stayed throughout the horrors of it by the same sort of faith in God.

But let us first see how her picture may be said to emerge in the Gospels. The place to start is probably the astonishing story at the end of chapter 7 of Luke, with Jesus out to dinner. A woman, unaccompanied, unannounced, uninvited (and from the point of view of the host, thoroughly unwelcome), somehow gets into the dining area of the house, stands behind Jesus where he reclines to eat, weeps all over his feet (perhaps feet in desperate need of attention) and wipes them with her hair (perhaps unbound, perhaps bound up as a sort of towel). Then she soothes them with an expensive ointment, for she brings it in an alabaster jar. The host is scandalized, as well he might be, and uses the occasion to think ill of Jesus, who spots that he is doing so, and gives him a stinging rebuke on the woman's behalf. The text reads as though she already knew him and he her, hence her overwhelming gratitude and her trust in Jesus' capacity to reassure her of God's forgiveness for her sins – whatever they were. Being labelled as a 'sinner' does not necessarily mean that she was the prostitute of later imagination. If, however, she was a prostitute, we might bear in mind that she may have had starving children to feed, like many others in different times and circumstances, including our own. She is unnamed, but has been given a name because of what follows in the text, where we find a list of women, with her name first – a group healed of 'evil spirits and diseases' and now accompanying the disciples with Jesus. After all, footloose preachers need places to rest, clean up, eat, attend to sore feet and minor injuries. Is Mary, named first of the group, the same as the woman who wept over his feet in the previous passage? If you were an Orthodox Christian you would think not.

The Orthodox never recall her as a penitent, nor do they identify her with one or more of the other Marys of the Gospels.
Apart from 22 July they honour her as one of the women
bearing myrrh, two weeks after their celebration of Easter.
The Western Church has taken a different view because of
sermons preached by Pope Gregory I at the turn of the sixth/
seventh century. Identifying one Mary with another or with
an unnamed woman helps to build up a good story and she
becomes a model of penitence and the receipt of forgiveness.
One can readily appreciate her as one who had discerned how
the boundless mercy of God could transform a life – and at
that she was a saint for men as well as women. She became a
source of inspiration of a quite unexpected kind, which we can
see if we reflect on another perplexing incident, in Luke 10,
where Martha is as critical of Jesus and Mary's relationship
to him as his host had been on a previous occasion. Martha's
abode may well have been one of the stopping-off places so
much needed by Jesus and his companions, and Martha herself
may exemplify all the virtues of the woman praised in the last
chapter of the book of Proverbs – that is, one whose price is
above rubies for the way she runs her household and the family
businesses. On this occasion Mary is simply not aligning herself with Martha and her responsibilities, but is 'sitting out',
we may say – sitting at Jesus' feet like any other (probably
male) disciple. Jesus maddeningly approves of what she is
doing – no comfort to Martha. With this incident in mind we
may discern a reason for the Oxford and Cambridge colleges
bearing her name, providing of course that there are enough
'Marthas' around to make life possible for those inspired by
Mary on this occasion.

So far, we can see why on the one hand Mary was honoured
as a disciple, and on the other why later ages set up Magdalen
homes or institutions for what were thought to be problematic
girls and women, not to mention her role as patron saint of
perfumers and hairdressers! The latter derives from yet another
Gospel incident, in Matthew 26. Jesus is being given hospitality yet again, when an unnamed woman (one of those giving
him hospitality?) comes in and pours precious oil/ointment

on his head, thereby making him literally an 'anointed one', a 'Christos', *the* Christos, perhaps, but of a profoundly troubling kind. Is this what Judas betrayed? That Jesus has been identified as an anointed leader – prophet or king maybe? In any event, this time it is grumbling disciples who find her action thoroughly inappropriate – why not, after all, sell the oil and give the proceeds to the poor? It must have been precious indeed. I venture to think that the relationship between Jesus and this woman is so sensitive and perceptive that what Jesus commends in her action is indeed what she perhaps has already begun to fear even before he is clear about it – that is, if he continues to speak and behave as he does, his death is inevitable. Does he commend her action because she has made it possible for him to realize what it is she foresees? To say that she has anticipated the anointing not of his head so much as his body for burial is a terrifying prospect that his disciples will reject if they can, and they do indeed abandon him when they themselves are threatened. Mary/the unnamed woman does indeed become the one whom Jesus praised by saying that what she has done for him will be retold wherever the gospel is preached, so why not add her into the story of Mary of Magdala, devoted and faithful to the bitter end? Except that there was more to say.

There are other Gospel passages to which we might give our attention if we had time, not least the puzzling narrative in John 11, the raising of Lazarus – Mary of Magdala so to speak having moved to Bethany. The most important, however, is undoubtedly the encounter with the risen Christ in the garden (see John 21 – an anticipation of Paradise?), the inspiration for so much painting and poetry in meditation on the scene. For the encounter turns her into the messenger of Jesus' resurrection to the disciples, hence her titles of 'equal to the apostles' and 'apostle to the apostles' in church tradition – not that that has counted for a great deal in relation to women's capacity to preach or proclaim the resurrection down through the centuries! That apart, beyond the Gospels a tradition developed that had Lazarus, Martha and Mary becoming the evangelists of southern France, Mary indeed being portrayed with three halos – one of which is as a preacher. Visit Vézelay, for example, and you will find the tradition alive and well there!

So that, in outline, assembles some reminders of some features of the story of Mary of Magdala, who needs to be freed of some later grossly distorting and silly representations of elements of the traditions about her. Better to recall her as at least an exemplar of courage, fidelity, acute sensitivity to others, not least perhaps to Christ himself, and confidence in God's power to overcome and transform the worst in our world – a confidence as much needed in our time as in hers.

27

Ignatius of Loyola (31 July)

I begin with a quotation from a Spanish poem in a nineteenth-century English translation. The last section runs:

Not with the hope of gaining aught,
Nor seeking a reward;
But as Thyself hast loved me
O ever loving Lord.

Even so I love Thee, and will love,
And in Thy praise will sing,
Solely because Thou art my God,
And my eternal King.[1]

I have chosen to begin with this poem because it is attributed to Francis Xavier, one of the original band of six companions of Ignatius of Loyola, who died on 31 July 1556. Both of them came from the same part of Spain – Navarre, in the Basque region. Ignatius was born in 1491 in the family castle of Loyola, adapting his Spanish baptismal name to that of Ignatius, an early Christian saint. We know about him in the first instance from his own account, more or less dictated in three sessions between 1553 and 1555 to a young Jesuit when in Rome – an account given somewhat reluctantly. The account begins with Ignatius' battle injury in 1521, when he was carried home with badly broken legs to endure months of treatment to get back on his feet. Bedridden, he had time to reassess his past life and to think about his future. And he began to draft what became his

---

1 *New English Hymnal* (Norwich: Canterbury Press, 1986), no. 73.

'Spiritual Exercises' – of which more later. As soon as he was able, he set off dressed as a vagrant in sackcloth, begging his food and resources, travelling to Jerusalem, from whence the Franciscans sent him back to Spain. There he began a ten-year course of study in various places, concluding in Paris in 1534. His was an age of 'reformation' and humanism, well supplied with heresy hunters, and with horizons transformed by overseas discoveries and associated trading and conquest. It is not surprising that he was sometimes regarded with suspicion – he was dressed neither as a Dominican nor a Franciscan (the other mendicants being in proper orders); he was without authority to preach and to teach and to offer his 'Spiritual Exercises' – it was in Salamanca in 1527 that we have the first written indication of their existence. Members of the Society of Jesus all start with these in their 30-day retreat at the beginning of a training that may last up to 14 years – a far cry then as now from the education of many (though of course not all) clergy.

While in Paris Ignatius gained his MA degree in 1534, the year in which he and his six companions, most of them much younger than himself (one was Francis Xavier with whom we began), made their commitment to one another – the start of the Society of Jesus. At this time Ignatius completed his 'Spiritual Exercises'. Let me (as a non-expert!) briefly indicate what these are about. First, Ignatius wanted them to aid those on a retreat – with the assistance of a guide – to immerse themselves in their faith so that they could choose their life-course in accordance with what could be discerned about the will of God for them, and to make that choice *in inner freedom*. Second, he encouraged people to *use their imagination* in respect of the Gospel texts – take a reference to Jesus at a meal, for instance, and place yourself there in imagination. Third, he encouraged the conviction that everything could be done for the *greater glory of God*, even the smallest thing – *Ad maiorem Dei gloriam*, AMDG for short. And fourth, he wanted everyone to see God living in his creatures – any and all of them. Since the focus of the new Society was to be mission, it is unsurprising to find Jesuits studying just about everything between them – sciences, arts, languages, technologies, social justice, not least in endeavouring to understand, value and appreciate the cultures of those they hoped to convert. In time, they were to be found worldwide, sometimes in collision with both those exploiting the worlds new to them, whether ancient civilizations or indigenous peoples (of which the film *The Mission* gives a glimpse) and sometimes in profound disagreement with other religious orders.

The first draft Constitution of the Institute was drawn up in 1539, and with revision soon received papal approval, partly perhaps because those enlisted in the 'militia of Jesus Christ' (crack troops?) were to be obedient to Christ's vicar on earth, bypassing the bishops – which hardly made them more popular. They were to advance the understanding of Christian life and doctrine by the ministry of the word, by spiritual exercises, works of charity and the instruction of children and the uneducated, and with an eye out for talented students who might join these 'soldiers of God'.

The ongoing history of the Jesuits is one of controversy, even of suppression from time to time, and martyrdom – for example, under National Socialism in the twentieth century in Europe and in Latin America. But for us, in our own time, we have much to be grateful for in their gift to the worldwide Church of an extraordinary line of theologians, and of the first Jesuit pope, Francis. And we have another cause for gratitude which I sketch here only very briefly. In the early part of the seventeenth century, an enterprising Yorkshirewoman, Mary Ward, was so impressed with what she had learned of the Jesuits that she found in them the inspiration for her own vocation and that of her friends, disregarding every convention and expectation of how women were to behave. She refused enclosure, refused special clothing, insisted on freedom to move wherever her companions were needed across continents, in their determination to educate girls of all classes – poor girls included. It may now seem extraordinary, given her story, that she and her companions were so persecuted, but they survived to set up what became the Institute of the Blessed Virgin Mary (IBVM), though they were not allowed to acknowledge her as their founder until 1909, by which time they were educating at least 70,000 girls in their schools worldwide. And, amazingly, in 2002 – at last – they were allowed to adopt the Constitution of the Jesuits as Mary Ward had wished, becoming themselves a Congregation of Jesus.

In my view, then, we owe a lot to Ignatius and those who joined him, and thank God for all of them, and pray for more vocations to the Society of Jesus from whom we have so much to learn.

28

Michael and All Angels
(29 September)

I think that first of all we might acknowledge that some feasts are, as it were, sent to try us. That is to say, they require us to focus on items of our tradition that we might not otherwise much bother with – a feast is one way of getting us to pay attention! The central point in the case of Michael and All Angels is to think, to imagine, how at the end of it all the created universe will manifest its utter dependence on its divine creator. That is, in a biblical worldview, angels serve the divine intentions for some kind of unimaginable fulfilment – like us, they are servants of God.

We slither so easily past or through the texts that could and should prompt us – not just once a year – to grasp a modest sense of our place in the scheme of things, in God's scheme, together with angels and archangels. For instance, recall the 'Gloria' of the heavenly host from Luke's Gospel; then the eucharistic invitation to join in with angels, archangels and all the company of heaven in what in our arrogance we are liable to think are our initiatives in praise of God – in the lead of all other creatures, as it were. Actually, the lead is always being taken elsewhere. It's like an 'open house' party in which we are invited to join – we didn't set it up. Then there are the words from Isaiah 6: 'Holy, holy, holy, is the Lord of hosts; the whole earth is full of his glory.' That is, not just that it looks good, but that the authority, the weight, the splendour of the Lord of the heavenly armies is manifest everywhere, did we but have eyes to see it. Familiarity, and beautiful musical settings of these words, however appropriate they may seem, can lull us into a kind of failure – the failure to think and imagine what it is to which we are committing ourselves when we use the language of angels and archangels, and what, allegedly, they get up to. They are not domesticated pets, after all.

Familiarity in worship apart, some of our difficulty may come from the association of angels with occasions where we rightly discern divine blessing, such as the gift of children (male children at any rate!). Think of the way in which the six-winged seraphs of Isaiah's awesome vision have been turned into plump little cherubs – delight and pleasure turned sentimental, and doing no justice to actual babies and their parents, least of all the dangers of childbirth to their mothers. Maybe they serve as a kind of consolation for the loss of children, but 'cherubic' images still distort Isaiah's vision and its significance. Divine blessing is not necessarily easy to deal with. The mysterious visitors to Sarah and Abraham's camp to promise a child to Sarah in her old age reduce her to laughter. There's the angel of the exodus, sometimes manifest as cloud or pillar of fire, which does not always inspire confidence on the long trek. There's the dealings of an angel with Manoah and his wife, resulting in the birth of Samson, an angel who half terrifies them, and who leaves them in the flames of their sacrificial offering. There's the annunciation of the angel to Mary (though with at least one painter having the angel kneel to her); there are the angelic instructions to Joseph, the angelic visitor to Zacharias in the temple. He might have laughed, like Sarah, or got it right, like Mary, but as a result of his challenge to the angel he ends up dumb for a time. Quite apart from the problems of the lives and sometimes dreadful deaths of these children of promise, sentimentality is not appropriate here. Manoah and his wife are rightly terrified by their messenger; Mary and Joseph are surrounded by menace, spending some time with their new-born as asylum seekers, migrants – no exodus angels for them. Isaiah in his vision sees seraphs, sizzling creatures of fire, one of whom cleans his mouth with a live coal. And insofar as they can be seen and have shape, they have six wings each – weird enough. Even stranger is the attempt made by Ezekiel to describe the living creatures who make up the great chariot of God – another aspect of angelic divine service. As Ezekiel wrote, 'their appearance was like burning coals of fire', fire and lightning. Holy angels bright indeed.

Sometimes we may come across a marvellous visual aid, as in the churches with surviving angel-roofs such as are to be found in East Anglia, though probably nowadays without the brilliant and gaudy colouring and decoration that helped to create the sense of the presence of angels and archangels partying away, or bearing the divine presence into a place of worship. Recall Peter Wimsey in Dorothy L. Sayers' novel *The Nine Tailors*, where Peter is to be found in a church at dead of night (seeing in the New Year) in an area surrounded by the miseries of floodwater. Peter settles into his pew, looks carefully around, then looks upwards: 'there, mounting to the steep pitch of the roof, his eyes were held entranced with wonder and delight. Incredibly aloof, flinging back the light in a dusky shimmer of bright hair and gilded outspread wings, soared the ranked angels, cherubim and seraphim choir over choir, from corbel and hammer-beam floating face to face uplifted. "My God", muttered Wimsey, not without reverence. And he softly repeated to himself, "He rode upon the cherubims and did fly; He came flying upon the wings of the wind"'[1] – Psalm 18's allusion to the divine chariot and to the divine presence borne by those angels.

No angel roof here, however. This is post-Reformation Scotland after all. But let us be as alert as we can to the presence of the angels in Scripture and liturgy – messengers, divine chariot and all, not just at the beginning of the Gospels but at critical moments within them, such as ministering to Christ in the desert; at his terrible ordeal in Gethsemane; mysteriously and in a sense most terrifying in and around his place of burial. Joy on the part of those encountered by them, but fear too in their reactions. And in John's Gospel, as we heard this morning, they are inescapably part and parcel of understanding the divine presence in the person of Jesus, with that amazing image

---

1 Dorothy L. Sayers, *The Nine Tailors* (London: Hodder and Stoughton, 2016), 32.

of angels legging it up and down a ladder to the gate of heaven in Jacob's dream – an image now attributed to Jesus himself, promising that the gate of heaven will be opened, with Jesus himself the means by which the angels ascend and descend. Strange stuff indeed, reinforced by the extraordinary images we find in the book of Revelation. The crucial section is concerned with Satan's defeat – Satan an angel created good and gone to the bad, and not allowed to get away with his wickedness. Recall the great image of his defeat on the outside of Coventry Cathedral.

So in the biblical view we may say that this is why these weird and terrifying angels and archangels are important. It is not as the divine chariot, or just as messengers to human beings, but central to the divine battle against evil. Have another look at Daniel 7 sometime when the news of utter brutality and sheer horror and cruelty seems to be overwhelming as it is transmitted to our screens. Daniel 7 apart, try praying 'angels and ministers of grace defend us' (Hamlet); or use one of this morning's splendid hymns. Or recall an angelic name: Gabriel as 'man of God', perhaps the most suitable messenger to human beings; Raphael (God has healed); and principally Michael, whose very name is a sort of warning to us in the form of a question. For 'Michael' means 'Who is like God?' – to which the only response is of course 'no one'. The implication is that all praise is due to God – 'all things come of thee and of thy own do we give thee'. Michael's name reminds us that our loyalty is ultimately to God (not a president, a monarch, a nation, a party leader or whatever), even, ultimately, beyond our nearest and dearest, our precious and life-giving intermediate loyalties, as it were. For God at the end of it all is the one who will wipe away all tears, when as the book of Revelation has it, 'there shall be no more death, neither sorrow, nor crying, neither shall there be any more pain' (Revelation 21.4–5, KJV); when in divine justice and mercy everything will indeed manifest the divine glory, the state of affairs in the biblical vision that the angels and archangels help to bring about.

29

Francis of Assisi (4 October)

As many of you will know, several members of the congregation have connections with Anglican Franciscan communities – communities that after a long absence after the Reformation era began again in the United Kingdom around the turn of the twentieth century, though the Franciscan tradition does not seem to have bitten very deeply into the Scottish Episcopalian psyche, except perhaps at All Saints in St Andrews and Old St Paul's in Edinburgh. But since on 4 October the Church worldwide commemorates Francis it seemed to me a good moment to remind ourselves of some features of his story of sanctity. I say some features, because he was such an entrancing figure who captured the hearts of so many that all sorts of traditions about him grew up even during his lifetime, let alone beyond. No one else inspired anything comparable to those wonderful pictures by Giotto which still fire the imaginations of those who see them in Assisi.

Born in 1181 in Assisi, he was baptized John but commonly known as Francis, perhaps after his mother's homeland. It may have been his mother who taught him many of the French songs that sustained him in dire circumstances. His father was a prosperous cloth merchant – a business in which Francis had not a shred of interest except insofar as it supplied him with resources. These included smart military kit for an expedition against Perugia, which came to an end for Francis and the rest of the young company he was in when they were imprisoned in foul conditions, awaiting ransom. It was from this time that some of his countrymen thought he was a fool – singing entertaining songs in the midst of such discomfort and misery. And also, even more surprisingly, treating everyone he had dealings with with astonishing civility and courtesy. Ransom from his father came, but not before Francis had contracted a grim fever from which he never fully recovered.

The years 1204 to 1206 were the period of his conversion, which did nothing to reconcile him to his father. On another expedition he gave his kit to an impoverished knight, and backed out of the company he was in. On a pilgrimage to Rome he exchanged clothes with a destitute pauper and began to beg for food. Francis was beginning to fall in love with his favourite lady, Lady Poverty. There were of course precedents for this sort of behaviour of which he may well have been aware – similar stories were told of Martin of Tours. But there was another bit of the Martin story Francis still had to come to terms with, and that concerned those with leprosy. People suffering with what we now call leprosy or some other disfiguring skin disease that exiled them from other human company were among the most feared of outcasts. But on meeting one such man near home, Francis found the courage and compassion to embrace him, then, turning around as he continued on his journey, he found that the man had vanished. The care of such outcasts was to mark his followers for generations.

Was this his first encounter with Christ in person? He soon experienced one such encounter about which he could not be mistaken, when the image of the Crucified One in the almost ruined chapel of San Damiano actually spoke to him and instructed him to repair his house, which Francis took to mean the chapel itself. He went about it in completely the wrong way, selling a bolt of expensive cloth that was of course the property of his father, and then finding that no one would touch the money for the rebuilding. His father had had enough by this time, and locked Francis up at home, but he was released by his mother in his father's absence. When his father returned, he took Francis first to the local magistrates' court, and when Francis claimed the protection of the church, hauled him before the local bishop, Guido. This time, Francis had to do what he was told – return the money to his father. Then he caused further offence by tearing off his smart clothes, again, but this time throwing them at his father's feet and declaring that he had no earthly father, but only one Father who was in heaven. No courtesy to his father, apparently. At some point afterwards Francis found something to wear – something like old sacking perhaps. If you think of the texture of the fabric of a jute shopping bag it was probably as rough as that. He hitched a piece of rope round his middle, and took off to live rough, to scavenge and beg for his food. What might this have looked like to his contemporaries? Here's G. K. Chesterton on the subject:

> A young fool or rascal is caught robbing his father and selling goods which he ought to guard; and the only explanation he will offer is that a loud voice from nowhere spoke in his ear and told him to mend the cracks and hollows in a particular wall. He then declared himself naturally independent of all powers corresponding to the police or the magistrates, and takes refuge with an amiable bishop who is forced to remonstrate with him and tell him he is wrong. He then proceeds to take off his clothes in public and practically throw them at his father, announcing at the same time that his father is not his father at all. He then runs about the town asking everybody he meets to give him fragments of buildings or building materials, apparently with reference to his old monomania about mending the wall. It may be an excellent thing that cracks should be filled up, but preferably not by somebody which is himself cracked; and architectural restoration like other things is not best performed by builders who, as we should say, have a tile loose. Finally the wretched youth relapses into rags and squalor and practically crawls away into the gutter.[1]

As Chesterton concludes: 'That is the spectacle that Francis must have presented to a very large number of his neighbours and friends.' And we may add, it must have been misery and agony for his family.

---

1 G. K. Chesterton, *St Francis of Assisi* (London: Hodder and Stoughton, 1923), 75.

Between 1206 and 1213 Francis changed, and thus changed the minds of those who encountered him. First of all, he was joined by two other men, one a solid citizen and the other a churchman – Bernard and Peter – and they lived in a hut near a leper hospital whose patients they did something to serve. They were inspired by Francis' literalism as he read the Gospels in February 1208 or 1209; sell all you have and give to the poor; move around to preach and take no resources with you; and be prepared to carry a cross, like Christ. Here was the foundation of what eventually became the Franciscan Rule – a full version of which was eventually accepted by the papacy, which in any case shrewdly gave approval to Francis' venture. For he and his two companions became great preachers of the gospel, and it was living what he preached, dramatizing it, acting it out as we might say, that brought about his transformation. So Francis became exuberant with joy not only about how he was living and what he was doing for and with other human beings, but in praise of God and each and every creature he came across, particularly the injured or those to be rescued from slaughter. For him each and every creature was a source of delight – embraced in that famous episode of his preaching to the birds – an opportunity to praise them, as well as to remind his listeners to praise the God who had made them, and enjoining one and all to sing the gospel. For a time, there seems to have been a falcon who acted as his alarm clock, and who knew when the saint was so tired it was better to let him sleep in. And perhaps as a scavenger himself Francis was quite the best placed to negotiate rations for the wolf of Gubbio who had made a nuisance of himself in his search for food. Francis particularly loved the Feast of the Nativity, and even if he was not the very first, it was to Francis very largely that we owe the dramatization of Christmas with kings and angels and shepherds in costume, animals standing at the crib with Mary and Joseph and the Child. And on Christmas Day it was the responsibility of the well-off to feed both beggars and birds and provide extra feed for working animals. He lived the drama of the Gospels as much as he could.

He managed to upset another family, however. Clare of Assisi had heard of Francis' renunciation of worldly goods when she was just 12 years of age; when later she heard him preach, in 1211, she sought his advice, and he and his small company arranged to sweep her up, change her clothes and shoes, cut her beautiful hair, put a black veil on her head, and take her to safety in a nearby Benedictine house. Much family upset inevitably ensued, but eventually a sister and her mother were to join her in the new form of life to which she committed herself. Of course, this was not the radical footloose existence of Francis and his growing company, but the more familiar form of enclosure especially for women. For Francis, Clare was the most Christ-like person he knew. She herself became an exceptional 'religious', and by the time of her death in 1253 – years after her beloved Francis – there were over 150 communities for women in Francis' Second Order. She was publicly recognized as a saint shortly afterwards (the story of the Third Order cannot be told here).

Unfortunately for Francis personally, however, his very gifts created significant difficulties. First three companions, then 12, and in ten years maybe 3,000–5,000 of them, as at the famous Chapter of the Mats in 1221 – a great gathering camped out in rush-made huts and shelters, provided with food and drink by the local populace. This may at one level have been a sign of the appreciation of the Friars Minor, the Little Brothers as they had become known, but it also warded off the danger of having so great a number on the hunt for supplies through the neighbouring settlements. Francis had come back from a great journey to Syria and the hideous world of the Crusades, which rightly appalled him, having failed to convert the Sultan commanding an army opposing the Christian marauders. In that context, he had preached the peace of Christ. He had also visited the great university at Bologna, where he found that some of the Little Brothers had already moved into the world of salaried university teaching – anything but what was encompassed in Francis' vision. There really were some serious issues at this point. How was Francis' vision and practice to find its home in the new Europe coming into being – including its new towns and universities? Were the Friars to have permanent buildings in which to live? Were they to own them? Maintain them? How were they to eat? What resources were they to have at their disposal? Why not live as hermits, or footloose and on the move?

At the Chapter of the Mats Francis offered a revised Rule, appealing to Lady Poverty above all – but basically at this point he left them all to it. He was getting tired; he could eat very little after years of being at least half-starved; he had recurring fever, he was going blind and suffered some appalling treatment for his eye complaint. A man sympathetic to the Little Brothers gave him a lump of Mount Averna, known for its atrocious weather, and in 1226 Francis withdrew there with just three companions, at least one of whom had been with him from the very beginning. This period lasted from the Feast of the Assumption (15 August) to the Feast of St Michael and All Angels (29 September). He asked to be left alone in a hut, supplied with bread and water just once a day. There he had the overwhelming experience of seeing one of those seraphs from the angelic hierarchy somehow bearing the image of the crucified Christ. And as a grace or gift – or affliction – Francis received the marks of the Crucified One, the stigmata, in his hands, feet and side. As he wanted to live the gospel, indeed he received it. He could no longer use his hands, he needed constant nursing and bandaging of his wounds, and of course he could no longer walk. He had left his litter back in Assisi only to be laid on the bare earth for his death after evening prayer on 3 October 1226, when he sang a line from Psalm 142.7: 'Bring my soul out of prison, that I may praise your name.' He left not only his Little Brothers, but the whole Christian world, one quite remarkable legacy, completed right at the end of his life in the midst of all his suffering. This was the Canticle of Brother Sun, or the Canticle of the Creatures. He wrote a melody that the Brothers were to sing together after preaching their sermons to anyone who would listen. It happens to be the earliest example of lyric poetry in Italian. For us, what matters is that we are invited to glimpse something of Francis' spirit as we sing a version of it – 'All creatures of our God and King'.

Perhaps we might turn to it when things are at their worst for us, as surely Francis did at the end of a life that began in some turmoil and ended in sanctity.[2]

---

2 See the very cautious Dominican 'sanctoral' for the feast of St Francis: 'In a hermitage, a man who had the appearance of a Seraph who was as if hanging on the gibbet of the cross appeared to him and impressed into his hands and feet scars that were like nail marks, while on his right side there appeared the scar of a wound produced by the lance which had pierced it.' André Vauchez, *Francis of Assisi* (Newhaven, CT: Yale University Press, 2012), 365 note 52.

30

Elizabeth Fry (12 October)

From the cluster of commemorations at this time I have chosen
Elizabeth Fry, the social reformer. When she died in 1845 in
Ramsgate (on 12 October), around 1,000 people gathered as
she was laid to rest in a Quaker burial ground. I have chosen
her not least because whether we like it or not some of her
concerns remain with us.

She was born in 1780 in Norwich into the Gurney family,
a well-connected group of philanthropists and bankers. Her
mother died when Elizabeth was only 12 years old (giving
birth to her twelfth child). The girls in the family seem to have
been well educated and all the children were imbued with sensitivity towards the less fortunate. Thus it was no surprise to
find Elizabeth herself as a child setting up a Sunday school
for poor children, otherwise lacking more than the most elementary education as they would have been out at work from
a very young age. Elizabeth became deeply critical of herself,
however: in a diary entry of August 1797 she wrote that her
inclinations led her to be 'an idle, flirting, worldly feeling girl'.
She enjoyed her clothes, singing and dancing, of all of which
she became much ashamed. She sobered up in time to marry
Joseph Fry in 1800, and would have had more than enough to
do given the birth of 11 children (five sons and six daughters),
only one of whom died, a little girl, at the age of five.

Elizabeth became known as a 'Plain Quaker' – one of the
most austere sort. And by her time, much had been forgotten
in general public consciousness about Quaker origins in the
mid-seventeenth century. In those early days they were justifiably seen as public nuisances, as they were not called Quakers

(or Shakers) for nothing – Spirit-filled and challenging their supposed social and political superiors with liberal quotations from the most threatening parts of the book of Revelation. By the beginning of the nineteenth century they were still something of a challenge, with their plain dress, plain speech, holding meetings at least an hour in length in deeply attentive silence, unless someone under divine inspiration was driven to speak. Holding that no intermediaries between human persons and the divine were necessary, their places of worship were exceptional in their simplicity. The Quakers themselves, however, undoubtedly retained vivid recollections of the persecutions to which they had been subjected, with experience of imprisonment familiar enough. When change in legislation allowed they came to speak and serve as the embodied consciousness of their society, which was far from easy in an era when revolution was abroad, inevitably much feared at home, and with political dissidents regarded as especially troublesome – a familiar enough story.

Notwithstanding the demands of marriage and child-rearing, by 1811 Elizabeth was recognized by Quakers as one of their 'ministers', insofar as that makes sense given their traditions. In theory if not always in practice, women could and did speak at Quaker meetings – being bearers of 'inner light' as were men. For them as for other women, it was a different matter if they wanted to use their voices outside meetings, for that was 'not done' for 'respectable' women, instantly identifiable as they were by their speech and dress. Undeterred, Elizabeth Fry both used her voice in public and exercised her very considerable managerial talents in respect of a number of concerns. Over her lifetime she was involved in setting up shelters for the homeless, and where possible helping them back into work. She set up shelters for discharged prisoners, and homes and education for children, years before organizations such as the Society for the Prevention of Cruelty to Children and any systematic effort existed to provide for the homeless. She understood the importance of vaccination against smallpox and had her own children vaccinated as an example. She concerned herself with what were known as 'lunatic asylums'; she set up a School for

Nurses at Guy's Hospital – some of those trained there would go with Florence Nightingale to the Crimea.

Her major concern, for which she is best known, was with the state of prisons, especially those prisons housing women and children, in a state of filth, violence and general degradation hardly known to most people. Her predecessor in the eighteenth century had been John Howard, but she was the first to preoccupy herself specifically with women and children. She became expert in using her connections to bring conditions in prisons to the attention of those who needed to know; for instance, one of her brothers-in-law was Thomas Buxton, an MP who could vouch for her personally when needed to do so. It was Newgate prison in particular that drew her attention, since it housed women awaiting trial as well as those serving terms of imprisonment and those sentenced to transportation, or public execution outside the prison (the Old Bailey is on the site of Newgate, and includes a statue of Elizabeth Fry). It is clear that one of her most fundamental convictions of which she tried to convince the prisoners was that if she and other citizens felt as they did for the prisoners, how much more must this be true of God in Christ, given Christ's own suffering as a prisoner and a hideous public execution. She sat those condemned to death at the front of her prayer meetings, and so far as was permitted accompanied those on their route to execution. (Hanging could be the penalty, for example, for forging money or for theft.)

What began as an Association (mostly of Quaker women) for the Improvement of the Females in Newgate, providing clothing, education, employment, knowledge of the Scriptures, and the habits of orderliness that might turn them into women sufficiently respectable to be able to gain employment, became the model for others throughout England and Scotland, and gained the support of Queen Victoria. Mrs Fry drew up rules that the prisoners had to agree to and adopt. Her scheme was so successful that in 1835 she was able to address both a House of Commons Parliamentary Committee and one in the House of Lords on the state of prisons. There was one particular horror still to address, which was the sentence of transportation.

Until Mrs Fry took action, the night before prisoners were to be moved to a transportation ship was a particularly terrible experience, given the knowledge of what they would face in the morning. Mrs Fry was able to achieve a measure of calm and order, in place of riots and damage, helping the prisoners to organize themselves into the required groups of 12, with their own 'space', with a 'monitor', in which they would live together on their ship (children up to the age of seven travelled with their mothers). She managed to have them taken from prison free of handcuffs and shackles, and stopped the practice of them being dragged into open wagons and paraded through the streets where they were at the mercy of abuse from the crowds. Free of restraint (and shackles were eventually made illegal), they were moved in closed carriages to the ships. Moreover, each prisoner was provided with a bag that contained a few items of clothing, a comb, a knife and fork, a Bible, spectacles if required, a ball of string, and the wherewithal to make patchwork quilts on the voyage; these might be sold at ports on the journey, or on arrival. More difficult was to secure knowledge of the destination of the prisoners, where they were to live and how they were to earn their livings in Australia.

That is the sketch. What might it make us attend to? Some suggestions: as far as I know, the United Kingdom is the only country in the European Union in which people (including 'unaccompanied minors') can be detained indefinitely. No wonder that in 2013 there was a parliamentary enquiry into asylum support for children and young people, and it makes shocking reading if you look it up on the web. The conclusion of the enquiry was that successive governments have most shamefully failed children and their asylum-seeking families, denying them the resources they need. One thing we can be proud of in Scotland is that on 1 October 2015 the Human Trafficking (Scotland) Bill was passed, which pledges that children arriving in Scotland separated from their families will be given an independent advocate to advise and assist them.

If we need a reminder of why these children matter, we might recall the Scottish Episcopal Church's policy statement about the Protection of Vulnerable Groups, which asserts that children are to be awarded special protection because of their vulnerability. 'They are to be respected as persons in their own right, created and loved by God. We therefore, commit ourselves to take all steps within our power to keep children and young people safe from physical, sexual and emotional harm.' In that light, what might Mrs Fry's story suggest to every one of us, believing as she did that 'the first duty of our lives is to be conformed to God's will and live to his glory'.

31

Teresa of Avila (15 October)

It is sometimes worthwhile to look at the days before and after a particular Sunday to see what or whom the doctrinal or liturgical experts of the Church suggest we should be commemorating. After all, we live in an ecumenical age, and probably need to know far more than we do about the traditions of other branches of the Christian Church. So this morning, we are going to attend briefly to Teresa of Avila, whose life spanned much of the sixteenth century (1515–82), adopted as Patron of Spain in 1617, canonized in 1622; and a long time afterwards, in 1970, made a Doctor of the Church – the Roman Catholic Church that is, and one of very few women to have received that endorsement. She is a particularly interesting example of someone whose life story is anything but one of calm progress and easy achievement. In her *Life* – part her own autobiography and part her writings on prayer – she left on account of her struggles and hard-won discernment of what, at least to her and to those who follow her, should be at the centre of attention of those who live the kind of life in which the practice of prayer of a particular character could be sustained.

Teresa was born on 28 March 1515, as carefully recorded by her adored father in the book in which he kept such family records. The family had to appear scrupulously Christian, since a grandfather was a convert from Judaism and, like others so placed, both he and his descendants could be vulnerable to malicious gossip that they were secretly still attached to the Jewish faith and sustained some of its traditions at home. Her father was a widower under the age of 30, with a couple of children alive from his first marriage, when he married Teresa's mother, herself aged only 14, and a somewhat sad figure in

Teresa's memory. A beautiful woman to begin with, she faded over the years until her death at only 33, exhausted by the birth of children, their care and household management. She did not really share fully in her husband's life, taking refuge in romantic tales of which he disapproved, while his reading matter was far more serious. It comes as something of a shock to learn that the young children in this family were introduced to tales of martyrdom, not so much those of a remote Christian past, but at the hand of Moors, so recently driven out of Spain. These so captured the imagination of the five-year-old Teresa that she persuaded one of her little brothers to slip out of the house with her early one morning to seek such martyrdom. Mercifully, they did not get very far – spotted by an uncle they were returned to the house and their distraught mother. But this was one of the stories about Teresa that were to capture the hearts and imaginations of her later readers. So, for example, the seventeenth-century poet Richard Crashaw writes in a hymn to her of Christ taking 'a private seat' and making his mansion 'in the mild and milky soul of a soft child'.

> Since 'tis not to be had at home
> She'll travel for a martyrdom.
> No home for her, confesses she,
> But where she may a martyr be.
> She'll to the Moors ...[1]

Christ calls her back for what Crashaw calls 'a milder martyrdom' – grim though it was, as we shall discover. As it happened, in that same year, 1520, Martin Luther, in distant Wittenberg, publicly challenged the then pope. Teresa in her adult life refers to Lutheranism as something to be dreaded, though in very different ways and in quite different places. Both were at the forefront of reform.

Just 13 years old when her mother died, she had seen nothing in her parents' marriage to make her think that marriage was her own vocation but it took years for her to discover quite what that was. She endured long periods of serious illness, both when sent

---

1 John Ramsden Tutin, ed., *Richard Crashaw: English Poems* (London: George Routledge & Sons, 1900), 86.

away to school at age 16, and then – despite her father's wishes, and indeed against her own emotional inclinations – when she escaped to a convent at All Souls' tide in 1536. At one stage she was so paralysed it was thought she would die, and it took her three years to get back on her feet. The convent she joined may well have been typical – filled with girls and women who had nowhere else to go: wearing a habit but with their own jewellery; able to take regular visits out, which saved the expenses of feeding them; sleeping in dormitories if they arrived without a dowry, but with their own sort of flatlet if well to do, as in Teresa's case. She had a guest room in which a younger sister stayed until she married, and her own oratory which she could decorate as she liked and where she could hold small musical parties on a saint's day. Families visited regularly, bringing presents of food – one of the biggest problems for some of these communities was to avoid starvation. Teresa lived at the Convent of the Incarnation for 27 years, gradually becoming aware that there was something profoundly at odds with living in this way and trying to live a life of prayer. She was in a Carmelite house, an order of obscure origins from the twelfth century that took its inspiration from the austere life of hermits and others on Mount Carmel, but had long since collapsed into slackness in both the men's and women's communities. With the death of her father in 1543, no matter what care she gave to her other relatives (and care she did) Teresa gradually found her focus, which was the reform of her own Order – not the founding of a new one, but reformation from within. This eventually required new houses of Carmelites to be established, and by the time she was 43, in 1558, she had begun to assert what she thought was absolutely vital for the kind of life she and others should be living.

As might have been predicted, this caused uproar. In the eyes of ordinary townspeople, houses of strictly enclosed women devoted to a life of prayer could seem to be yet one more burden. Teresa wanted her reformed houses to be without endowment, and for those who entered not necessarily to have dowries. She wanted vocations, not money. But how were they to earn their keep – and what were they for? Their claim was that they were dedicated to prayer on behalf of preachers and teachers – the men of the Dominicans, the heresy hunters of the day, and the Society of Jesus, founded in 1540; both followed a Rule, both relied on alms, but were out and about, not confined, able to seek resources. Why could Teresa not live the Rule as it had been intended within the convent where she was? Was she not setting herself up to be superior to others? Who was she to tell her sisters in the Order what was wrong with the way they lived? When racked by doubt, as she was throughout her life, she threw herself on the grace and generosity of God. So in respect of reform, she claimed to have the authority of Christ himself for what she wanted. Teresa was passionately devoted to the humanity of Christ – Christ himself present to her, instructing her in quite unmistakable terms, even if she could not quite describe what that presence looked like. But he made his position clear to her and told her not to fear opposition; he engraved his words in her memory, helping her to remain calm and determined. Was she deluded? Was she tempted by the devil? Claiming a special authority for herself? Discrediting other sisters? Misleading her confessors?

She needed powerful support from the authorities of her Order, from the bishops, and the Dominicans and Jesuits. Once she had it, a house had to be bought in a new place, and with or without her direct involvement got ready for a small group of just 13 new inhabitants – a small group, like Christ and 12 disciples. She learned to bargain and pay bills, for roofs, drains, floors, windows, furnishings, and in August 1562 the first new house, dedicated to St Joseph, came into existence. By the time she died in 1582, 16 new houses – some of them for the men of her Order – had been founded. This had meant endless journeys, riding on a mule or in a mule-cart over atrocious roads, in all weathers, stopping off in appalling inns (and we might spare a thought for innkeepers having to accommodate a group of Carmelites turning up from nowhere!). Eventually it became easier when she was requested to found new houses by the General of the Carmelites himself, and later with the support of Philip II, no less. Her Carmelites were conspicuous, wearing a rough, home-spun habit, a white cloak, and hemp sandals. It is true that one of the ways in which they were distinguished from other Carmelites was by being known as Discalced – that is, shoeless – but Teresa as always took a very practical view of when to wear sandals and when not. Going barefoot through ice and snow was hardly sensible, for instance. All the travelling made her vulnerable to yet more criticism of course – so much for the life of enclosure, as her enemies pointed out.

But, she gathered some remarkable support from time to time. Her chaplain for a decade was a certain John – all five feet of him – who was committed to reform of the men's Order, but had been taken prisoner by those who opposed it. He was jailed in Toledo for nine months and beaten so badly that he carried the scars on his shoulders for life, but in the prison cell from which he eventually escaped he produced some most remarkable poetry and images of his experience of Christ. We know him as St John of the Cross, and a Doctor of the Church. By comparison with John's fate, Teresa was at least spared imprisonment, though sometimes she had to keep her head down in one of her houses and be less of a public figure – which of course gave her more time to write.

For she did have to defend herself. She was more or less required to write her Life, which was sent off to the Inquisition. It was cleared and returned for circulation. It is full of remarks about her inadequacies, her being female, her lack of education, her submission to the Church – she said all the right things to give herself cover, we might say. Of her other writings on prayer, her best known is perhaps *The Interior Castle*, written between June and November 1577. The title has its origin in Christ's words in St John's Gospel – in my Father's house there are many mansions – which in Teresa's case, writing in Spain, became the 'Castle' of her work, with its innermost room where God may meet the soul.

So much more could be said about her, but at least one thing we can take away from learning about this most extraordinary life, and that is the words found in her prayer book at the time of her death: Let nothing disturb you. 'Let nothing make you afraid. All things are passing. God alone never changes. Patience gains all things. If you have God you will want for nothing. God alone suffices.'

32

Martin Luther (31 October)

'Thou shalt love the Lord thy God with all thy heart, and with all thy soul, and with all thy mind'; 'Thou shalt love thy neighbour as thyself.' My primary concern this morning is not with this interchange between Jesus of Nazareth and some Pharisees except just to begin with. What were they up to? Trying to see if they could get Jesus to join them? Because, of course, he shares their commitments – love of God and neighbour. And no one could seriously expect him to answer except as he did. Any child who had sat in synagogue school and developed memory for Scripture learned by heart – by repetition from a rabbi – could have replied as Jesus did, with words straight out of the book of Deuteronomy. But what did the words mean in practice? Here Jesus differed from the Pharisees. The point is that if anyone did not know what the words might mean in practice, someone was (and still is) always ready to tell them, out of the best possible motives, and with the best possible intentions – which is what makes disagreements so acutely painful when the expression of the love of God and neighbour is at stake.

Suppose, however, that you live a long way from Galilee and Jerusalem, in a quite different time and place; you have no direct access to these words but have to rely on others to tell you, to advise you what they mean in practice, and you have no way of considering whether what you have heard is true and correct, and whether the advice is reliable. You can't check the basic text for yourself as you have neither the original language in which the text was written, nor access to a translation into your own common speech.

So, consider the situation in medieval Western Europe, where

177

the available text is in Latin – a language itself inherited from a different civilization centuries ago. You are entirely reliant on what you are taught by men who are fluent in Latin, informing you of what the words mean, and what they mean in practice. A further problem was that by the end of the first thousand years of the Church's history, the Western Church had largely lost contact with the churches of the Eastern Mediterranean and beyond, the original homelands of Christianity. There was no possibility of consultation and cross-checking, no way of discovering that others did not see things in the same way. Whatever the differences and difficulties of the Church in the East – which abounded – these were not the same as those in the Western Church. Left over from that first millennium were disputes about the Eucharist; about clerical celibacy; about the value of marriage; about the spiritual and temporal power of the Bishop of Rome (the pope) – and, in particular, could it seriously be believed that Christ had bestowed all power upon the pope, who then delegated it to the nobility. Not an exhaustive list, but the point is that there was much discussion, and plenty of eagerness for reform. For instance, Franciscans and Dominicans came into existence to serve the reform and renewal of the Church; they travelled around, they studied in different places, they exchanged ideas and information, and were as interested as any group in considering new perspectives and positions. And it was the religious orders that were primarily responsible for preaching and teaching.

One of the problems to be tackled was directly connected to the emergence – more by accident than design – of the patterning of life by seven sacraments, from baptism to end-of-life anointing, and with the sacrament of penance to negotiate the muddles, misapprehensions – accidental and deliberate – and harms human beings inflict on one another. How am I to understand what I have done, how serious was it both to myself and the person I harmed? I might be able to sort that out on my own; I might express my contrition, my sorrow, if I know the words of the Psalms – Psalm 51.1, 10–11, for instance: 'Have mercy upon me, O God, according to thy lovingkindness: according unto the multitude of thy tender mercies blot out my transgressions ... Create in me a clean heart, O God ... Cast me not away from thy presence' (KJV). But suppose that I am persuaded that I need to discuss what I have thought and said and done with someone trained to listen and competent to help. That person might be able to discern whether my contrition is enough for God, out of loving-kindness and tender mercies, to blot out my misdoings. Or must I also hear someone say, 'I absolve you' – clerical responsibility and power in just three words that in themselves became matters of contention. And suppose, further, that I know, and my confessor knows, that there are things I can do to put things right; or if I can't do them directly I will express my contrition in almsgiving, for instance. Look at Matthew 25: feed the hungry, give drink to the thirsty, hospitality to the stranger, clothing for the destitute, care for the sick and for prisoners – care for the bodies and persons of others. But what happens when this almsgiving gets into a financial tangle of a rather different kind? Suppose you have been taught that there's a store of merit, a sort of bank of grace, on which the pope or his ordained representatives can draw on your behalf. Suppose then that you can draw on this 'bank' and you will be given a kind of receipt or certificate. This will enable you to earn your salvation, put yourself right with God, and, further, lighten at least some of the penalty for your sins not just in this life but in the next in a state of purgation or cleansing. Even worse, what if this transaction becomes linked to a major building project, such as the rebuilding of St Peter's in Rome? And what effect did this have on individual persons? Confessors both experienced in themselves and discerned in their penitents profound anxieties, mistrust, terror and hatred of God – anything but confidence in a God of loving-kindness and tender mercies. Justice, yes – certainly needed, but it has to be sought in such a way that people can love God with heart and soul and mind and their neighbours as themselves.

So: one of the reasons for the determination to get the Scriptures into the vernacular – recall Wycliffe, Tyndall, Luther, to name only three – was that people could hear and read the Scriptures in English, Scots, German, Welsh, Spanish or

whatever, without being condemned to death either for trans-
lating them or for owning a Bible. People could begin to see
that there was something profoundly wrong with the way the
sacrament of penance was understood and practised, and how
much else was arguably mistaken. And someone had to act as
whistle-blower. That person, as we know, was an Augustinian
monk, a professor of biblical studies by the age of 28, able to
read the New Testament in the original Greek. Luther was a
reformer in an era of reform, though, as it turned out, at an
unpredictable and terrifying cost which we still have to deal
with in our own time, with occasional flickers of mild ecu-
menism. I think that Luther and those who faced a whole raft
of problems in the Western Church had no alternative but to
attempt to get things changed. And his fundamental motive?
He said that the Scriptures are 'the swaddling clothes and
the manger in which Christ lies – simple and lowly are those
swaddling clothes, but dear is the treasure, Christ, who lies in
them'.[1] Or in the words of a sermon on forgiveness, he wanted
his hearers to remember well that 'Christ our God desires of
us nothing else but that we should have a sure and confident
heart and trust in him.' That was what would make it possible
to love the Lord God with heart, soul and mind and our neighbour as ourselves, as Jesus of Nazareth had both lived and had
desired for others.

---

[1] Cited in Carter Lindberg, *The European Reformations* (Chichester:
Wiley, 2011), 68.

33

Margaret of Scotland (16 November)

In many church windows in Scotland, among a group of saints we find Queen Margaret, identified by her splendidly royal attire. Something as splendid she would have worn in her husband's court, her husband being Malcolm III, king in Scotland following time spent in Northumbria (his mother's place of origin) awaiting the demise of Macbeth. And there are many reminders of Margaret still with us, apart from her efforts to ensure that the splendour of her husband's court honoured Scotland's standing. What may come first to mind is Queensferry, one of her efforts to make pilgrimage to St Andrews easier; then there's Dunfermline where she was married and brought up the royal children, and where the youngest son, David I, was eventually responsible for the establishment of the abbey, housing what became her shrine when she too became the focus of pilgrimage. We know of her influence supporting the forms of Christianity to be found in Scotland in her day, while also aligning the Church here with the Western, Roman tradition for its major feast days. We can visit her chapel, the oldest surviving bit of Edinburgh Castle; we have even more tangible links of her devout life in the existence of her psalter, her precious gospel book – a pocket-sized selection of readings from the Gospels, re-identified as hers towards the end of the nineteenth century – and a life of St Cuthbert. Why Cuthbert?

Margaret's era is one where, despite all the invasions and disruptions and destruction characteristic of the time, something important signalling continuity with past religious tradition was to survive, and that was the cherished memory of earlier saints and the building of places where their bodily presence might be encountered. It was important to possess not just body or relics, but a text – a book about them that could be copied and given as a precious gift to those who would value it. After many years of carrying Cuthbert's body to escape from seaborne marauders, monks had arrived in Durham, and the Scottish royal household had a significant interest in what was going on there. It is possible that Malcolm himself was present, towards the end of his life on 11 August 1093, at the foundation ceremony of Cuthbert's burial place in what became Durham Cathedral. Alexander, one of Malcolm's sons, attended the opening of Cuthbert's tomb in 1104. When he became king a few years later, he honoured his father's wishes in summoning a certain Prior Turgot from his responsibilities with the religious community in Durham up to St Andrews to become bishop here. And it is from writings by Turgot that we learn about the life of Margaret: what was arguably most significant about her, what would commend her as a saint, long after her death at the age of only 46, which took place shortly after that of her husband, on 16 November 1093.

Prior Turgot was a Saxon from Lincolnshire and that may have helped render him particularly acceptable to Margaret, herself a member of the family of West Saxon royalty that struggled in vain to retain the authority of kingship in the turmoil of invasions. It is just possible that Turgot was among those who in 1067 found themselves seeking refuge, along with a company of royal refugees, including Margaret, who was 20 years old. She had been born in Esztergom in Hungary during an earlier exile of her family. After nine years back in England, educated probably in an abbey as well as at court, she found herself in flight once again, with that precious gospel book in her luggage, and this time with just one parent surviving – her mother, together with a brother and sister. More by accident than design, they ended up on Scotland's shores, where the eligible Margaret was eventually persuaded to marry Malcolm, who was by then a widower with two surviving sons. Margaret and Malcolm had six sons and two daughters, and the phrase 'a nursery of saints' came to be used of the whole brood because of Margaret's piety and the family's charity, not just within the household, but well beyond it.

It was Turgot who was asked by Margaret in person to take care of her children after her death. But it was probably not just Margaret Turgot he had in mind when he wrote about her life. For although the direct line of Saxon kingship failed in England, the family came to find themselves very much at the centre of life at court there. The principal character here is one of the two daughters of Margaret and Malcolm – Edith. She had some experience of life in England when packed off for her education to a very aristocratic religious house whose abbess was Aunt Christina. Not just education was the issue here, for very probably Malcolm and Margaret were determined to keep Edith safe from those who might well have their eyes on her for a marriage alliance. Edith hated every minute of her time in the abbey, and was brought back north in 1092, only then to find herself responsible for three of her brothers after the death of her parents the following year. Her group in full flight south included the nine-year-old David, and this time refuge in the Norman-English court, where Edith married Henry I in 1100. It was Edith, with responsibility above all for young David, who needed Turgot's writings about her mother. Turgot himself may have had his eye on the future recognition of Margaret's sanctity – like Cuthbert, her body and relics and a narrative of her life might all be important in the future.

To begin with we may note that Turgot's recollection of Margaret informs us how she kept her own head and that of the children, and even that of her husband, in the context of life at court. So Turgot wrote for Edith: 'You desire not only to hear about the life of the Queen your mother, who ever longed for the angelic kingdom, but also to have her life constantly before you in writing so that, although you were only slightly acquainted with her face, you may at least obtain a more perfect knowledge of her virtues.' Margaret had most specially asked Turgot that as long as he lived he would remember her in his prayers and at mass, as well as take care of her children, pouring out his affection on them. Above all, she asked, Turgot was to teach them to fear and love God, and never cease from instructing them. And at this point her instructions became more precise. For she asked, 'When you see any of them exalted to the height of earthly dignity, then at once, as a father or teacher, in the highest sense, go to him, warn, and when circumstances require it, censure him, lest, on account of a passing honour, he be puffed up with pride, or offend God with avarice or through the prosperity of the world neglect the blessedness of life eternal.' Such was Margaret's advice for help in staying both sane and good at court.

More than this, however, Turgot cherished Margaret for what he called her devotion to justice, piety, mercy and love, and quoted the book of Job to reflect on her: 'from my infancy mercy grew up with me, and it came out with me from my mother's womb'. For what Margaret required most of herself and her husband and the court – setting them an unequivocal example – was compassion for all those who needed protection, especially for the enslaved, for widows and orphans. Wherever she went, many of them 'flocked to her as they would to a most beloved mother, and none of these ever left her without being comforted'. Turgot gives one particularly moving instance of how she behaved. During the 40 days before Christmas and throughout the whole period of Lent she would rise at dawn to say the psalter, and nine destitute children would be brought to her so that she might feed them. He wrote: 'She ordered soft food, such as little children delight in to be prepared for them daily; and when the little ones were brought to her, she did not think it beneath her to take them on her knee and make little sups for them and feed them herself with the spoons of her own table.' As Turgot asked, 'What could be more compassionate than her heart? What more gentle to the needy?' That is just one example of her compassion given practical and memorable expression.

I think Turgot here put his finger on why Margaret's memory was so cherished, and why the movement for her recognition as a saint grew beyond the local. There was a papal enquiry about her to the bishops of St Andrews, Dunkeld and Dunblane in the middle of the thirteenth century, and a feast of St Margaret was established by 1249. So what for us on the run-up to Christmas? To say what I think may be all too familiar and obvious: I believe that some 25 per cent of children in St

Andrews and in Fife more generally are living in households of near poverty. I should think that all of us here are finding some way of honouring Margaret's memory by some sort of practical action on their behalf. As we know, big things can come from small beginnings – even from the mere recollection of a saint commemorated here in this very church.

To Conclude

34

Elizabeth Cady Stanton, d. 1902

The date is 12 November 1895 and the scene is the Metropolitan Opera House, New York. The occasion is a reunion of 'The Pioneers and Friends of Women's Progress', organized by the National Council of Women. This was a cosmopolitan, largely female gathering, as representative of all classes and conditions as possible, and they were focusing on the eightieth birthday of Elizabeth Cady Stanton, who sat on stage in front of a framework of flowers. The other principal guest was another campaigner for social and political justice, Quaker Susan B. Anthony, herself aged 75. These two had had many disagreements through the years, but were fundamentally of one mind in their focus on justice for women – not just women as socially well placed as they were, but those living unbelievably hard lives on the frontier, or in the great industrialized cities to which immigrants turned. And of course there were women from families freed from slavery – of which more in a moment. The two old ladies up front were skilled politicians. They had learned to speak in public despite much disapproval, mostly from the clergy (see 1 Timothy 2.12). They had organized meetings, petitions, lobbied those in government at whatever level. They had nothing to lose, but wanted to see more changes before they died, and were rightly exasperated both by the slow pace of change and by younger women who were by no means as radical as they were.

Most recently, in 1892, Mrs Stanton had delivered a speech in various places on 'The Solitude of Self', urging women to take responsibility for themselves, for their own consciences, for being self-sufficient, self-sovereign. She had been a widow since 1886, and this speech was a repeated 'wake-up' call to women. She had more up her sleeve. Just a fortnight after the gathering at the Opera House, many women were to distance themselves from her as a result of the publication of *The Woman's Bible*. To appreciate her position on biblical texts, we need to back-track over her life in outline to understand how it was that she published this book in her eighties.

Elizabeth was born into a well-to-do family in New York State of five boys and six girls. As was anything but unusual at the time, though, it was a tragic family too. All the boys died young – the last, aged 20, when Elizabeth was 11. Daniel Cady, her lawyer father, never really recovered from the loss of his sons, any more than could his wife, no matter what the achievements of this particular daughter. He let her tuck herself into his office as he listened to his clients, so she gained a remarkable introduction to the plight of women in particular. She attended classes in Greek set up for boys, given by the minister of their Presbyterian church. She emerged as the prize-winner of his class, and he was to leave her his Greek lexicon, grammar and commentary. He also taught her mathematics and chess. She was sent off to an excellent school for girls run by a head who put up with no nonsense about what girls were or were not capable of learning.

Apart from anything else, Elizabeth learned to hunt out information for herself which stood her in excellent stead throughout her life. But what then? Obviously, except for a few very determined women, marriage was likely. But the situation of married women on both sides of the Atlantic was simply dire. They lost their legal existence as particular persons (re-read 1 Corinthians 11), and even as single women or widows problems existed. For instance, in the criminal code 'he', 'his' and 'him' included women, for they could be arrested, tried and hanged, and there were no women jurors or lawyers to speak for them in court. On the other hand, 'he', 'his' and 'him' did not include women in the American Constitution, or in most civil or ecclesiastical law. Until things changed over the course of the nineteenth century, as change they eventually did, a married woman's access to her inheritance (unless legal 'settlements' were in place), to control the money she earned and the property she helped to maintain – all this was entirely dependent on her husband being the kind of man who recognized the monstrous injustice of the situation and behaved accordingly. If he turned out to be feckless, alcoholic and violent, he could reduce her and their children to semi-starvation and destitution – as could her eldest son, if on his father's death the family property went to him. The fundamental root of the problem was that the conception of women on which all this was based was deemed to be derived from the 'Word of God'. There was thus a huge task ahead to persuade both women and men that there was nothing inevitable about this situation, that it was not 'God's will' for them. One thing that became clear during the course of the century, however, was that apparently immovable situations and social arrangements could be made to change. The paradigm example was slavery – the abolition of both slave-trading and slave-holding, neither of which are explicitly condemned by the 'Word of God'.

Elizabeth Cady married Henry Stanton when she was 24, and did so without the support of her family, who did not think much of his prospects at the time. She was never afraid to make her choices and stick by the consequences. Henry was committed to the abolition of slavery, and part of their honeymoon trip was to attend the London Anti-Slavery convention in June 1840. Elizabeth received two shocks there. The first was the discovery that many of the clergy present objected to the presence of women delegates, who included women like Elizabeth who had already raised money to support abolition. Another distinguished American Quaker, Lucretia Mott, was also present. She kept on display at her home not the usual Bible but a copy of Mary Wollstonecraft's 1792 A *Vindication of the Rights of Women*. The convention settled down once it had been agreed – not by the women, of course – that they could remain if they sat in a partitioned-off part of the hall.

The convention provided a superb opportunity to network, and to get to know some of the men who joined them, such as the great William Lloyd Garrison. The second shock Elizabeth received was that her husband was a single-issue man. In other words, Henry campaigned for the abolition of slavery, but would not put that campaign in jeopardy, as he thought it would, by campaigning for the rights of women. Elizabeth was different, for she campaigned for any and every cause for justice and freedom. She was to face the difficulty of single-issue campaigning right through her life, not least in the organizations she herself helped to set up to fight for votes for women. The vote has huge symbolic significance, insofar as it signified that women had minds and wills of their own. There was a question about the extent to which women might be willing to go on caring for the males in their lives, and much energy had to be spent in reassurance that all would be well.

Elizabeth and Henry and three children moved out to an area called Seneca Falls, where another four children were born to them, all of whom survived. Elizabeth was prime manager of the whole economic unit on which the household with its servants and workers depended, as Henry was often away. From this base Elizabeth combined with others and organized for 19–21 July 1848 a packed Women's Rights Convention. From this they produced their Declaration of Sentiments and a list of what needed to be tackled, such as changes in the legal status of women, their access to education, and properly paid employment. A demand to be voters was a controversial matter which some women thought might damage the argument for the others, but Elizabeth got her way. But another shock was in store for women, for at the conclusion of the appalling Civil War in 1865 the decision was made – by men – that the word 'citizen' in the Constitution included all males, but not females. The 'males' included liberated slaves, immigrants who could not yet speak 'American' – they still had many hurdles to overcome in order to vote, but the basic point was clear.

Elizabeth, together with family members and friends, produced a three-volume *History of Woman Suffrage* between 1881 and 1886. (It took until 1920 in the USA for votes for some women to be conceded, two years after the change in the UK, again for only some women at that stage.) One daughter, Harriot, gave invaluable support to her mother's campaigns. Harriot had married an Englishman and lived in Basingstoke. She was thus able to provide her mother with a base in England as transatlantic crossings became easier. Elizabeth in her turn did a great deal to support campaigns in the UK, though predictably found the British hierarchy and aristocratic privilege particularly irritating and obstructive.

The other major project she had up her sleeve was *The Woman's Bible*, alert as she was not only to the production of the Revised Version, but also to new currents of thought that continued to point up how problematic were some of the biblical texts if taken literally, even when an agreed translation was produced. Like it or not, readers had to get used to a vastly extended time-frame for life on earth, including human life, and also to biblical criticism, and to the relation of biblical texts to other ancient literature. There were versions of the Bible for children, for immigrants, for Sunday school teachers and day school teachers. Why then not a version for women? To produce anything of this kind needed contributors with the right language skills, and who could still take the Bible seriously. But having seen and heard the Bible being used in support of slavery, one could hardly be blamed for refusing to have anything to do with Elizabeth's project. Others were relying on biblical insights to support the dignity of women, though some were terrified of what the all-male clergy might think, despite the fact that some denominations already had a few ordained women. And some thought that a critique of the Bible would damage the campaign for votes for women.

Undeterred, Elizabeth got a team together and they proceeded to cut out and paste into notebooks those passages that referred explicitly to women, and to write commentary only on those passages – around one-tenth of the whole, as it turned out. It was thus on the basis of that tenth that so much of women's situation – deemed to be necessarily subordinate to men, inferior, legal nonentities (except when 'criminals') – had been derived. So what resources, if any, did the Bible offer women? The dominant voice in the commentary was that of Elizabeth, but there were counter-voices too: the same passage would be read from a different perspective, including, inevitably, the 'Great Women of the Bible' theme. Some of the material 'on the first five books' was serialized in a journal, and Part 1 came out in book form just a fortnight after Elizabeth's birthday celebration in the Opera House in New York. The rest (Part 2, Joshua to Revelation) was published in 1898.

It was clear that those who produced *The Woman's Bible* had had a whale of a time. For instance: 'If Miriam had helped to plan the journey to Canaan, it would no doubt have been accomplished in forty days instead of forty years.' Further, what had Christ learned from that determined woman fighting for her child? What had he learned from the encounter about the importance of children in relation to the kingdom of God he proclaimed? Perhaps predictably given some of the intellectual currents of a post-revolutionary era, Jesus emerges as a leading radical, with the apostles seemingly responsible for teaching the inferiority of women – a conclusion impossible to avoid. When some denounced *The Woman's Bible* as the work of Satan, Elizabeth retorted that Satan was not on the committee that had produced the book! One minister, however, reviewing the book, made Elizabeth's point splendidly: 'There is nothing that is morally and philosophically so stupid and senile as the orthodox arguments for women's timeless and universal subjection to man.'

The Woman's Bible was thoroughly controversial and Elizabeth loved every minute of it. It was a publication success, with seven printings in six languages. It was rediscovered after World War Two, becoming a significant catalyst for biblical scholarship by women. It remains stimulating reading for its ideas and insights. I do not think I need labour the point about how some of Elizabeth Cady Stanton's concerns are still with us both inside and outside the churches. So let me conclude with some words of William Lloyd Garrison at the memorial meeting held after her death in 1902: 'For greater than to be the partisan of any one single cause, however noble, is it to maintain a vital interest in every effort for human freedom. It was the breadth of vision and inclusive sympathy which was the highest distinction of Mrs Stanton.'

Acknowledgements

A version of 'The Face of Christ' was previously published in Susan Durber and Heather Walton (eds), *Silence in Heaven: A Book of Women's Preaching* (London: SCM Press, 1994). Used by kind permission of SCM Press.

'Why Worship?' was previously published in *Il Illo Tempore: Ushaw Library Journal of Liturgical Review* 16 (2001). Used with kind permission of Ushaw Library.

'Word and Sacrament' was previously published as 'Word and Sacrament: Recovering Integrity', in Neil Brown and Robert Gasgoine, eds, *Faith in the Public Forum* (Adelaide: ATF Press, 2000). Used by kind permission of ATF Press.

A version of 'Catherine of Siena' was previously published as 'Consider Catherine', in *New Blackfriars: A Monthly Review of the English Dominicans* 77 (1996), 164–81. Used by kind permission of John Wiley and Sons.